T0268205

Higher Admissions

OUR COMPELLING INTERESTS

AN INITIATIVE OF THE
UNIVERSITY OF MICHIGAN
WITH SUPPORT FROM THE
ANDREW W. MELLON FOUNDATION

Earl Lewis and Nancy Cantor, Series Editors

Other books in this series:

Gary Orfield,
> *The Walls around Opportunity: The Failure of Colorblind Policy for Higher Education*

Eboo Patel,
> *Out of Many Faiths: Religious Diversity and the American Promise*

Scott E. Page,
> *The Diversity Bonus: How Great Teams Pay Off in the Knowledge Economy*

Earl Lewis and Nancy Cantor, editors,
> *Our Compelling Interests: The Value of Diversity for Democracy and a Prosperous Society*

Higher Admissions

The Rise, Decline, and Return of Standardized Testing

Nicholas Lemann

PRINCETON UNIVERSITY PRESS

PRINCETON & OXFORD

Published by Princeton University Press
41 William Street, Princeton, New Jersey 08540
99 Banbury Road, Oxford OX2 6JX

press.princeton.edu

Library of Congress Control Number: 2024932880

ISBN 9780691246765
ISBN (e-book) 9780691246772

British Library Cataloging-in-Publication Data is available

Editorial: Eric Crahan, Rebecca Binnie
Production editorial: Elizabeth Byrd
Jacket: Katie Osborne
Production: Danielle Amatucci
Publicity: Alyssa Sanford (US); Kathryn Stevens (UK)
Copyeditor: Ashley Moore

Jacket Credit: dule964 / Adobe Stock

This book has been composed in Arno Pro

Printed in the United States of America

10 9 8 7 6 5 4 3 2 1

Contents

Commentary: The Multiple Lives and Ironies
of the SAT

Prudence L. Carter

Higher Admissions

Introduction

By Series Editors Earl Lewis
and Nancy Cantor

TESTING DEFINES LIFE for scores of students in the United States. According to a 2015 study by the Council of the Great City Schools, students take on average 112 standardized tests between kindergarten and when they graduate high school.[1] While the study focused on young people in large urban districts, the sense that testing occupied hours per year held true for students in all districts. Some of these tests are formative, assessing progress and comprehension of a subject during a period of instruction. Other tests are summative and provide feedback after the period of instruction has ended. As Nicholas Lemann notes in this volume, over the last three generations one summative test has been elevated to national importance, the SAT—although in some states and communities the ACT has emerged as a competitor. Once called the Scholastic Aptitude Test, and now simply the SAT, this test has played a fundamental role in sorting the nation's talent for more than seventy-five years. In the process we came to link success on the test with merit. This book and its comments call that logic into question.

The SAT first saw prominent use as a tool to democratize entrance into the nation's Ivy League institutions. James Bryant Conant, president of Harvard University, worried that young men (it would be a generation before young women were included) who had not attended eastern boarding schools had a disadvantage when it came to taking the period's College Board admissions exams. As a remedy, in the 1930s Conant, in partnership with Henry Chauncey, an assistant dean at Harvard, advocated for the adoption of the SAT, an adapted IQ test that had been developed experimentally by the College Board in the previous decade. The pair envisioned an admissions test that would allow them to move beyond the traditional candidate pool. In 1947 Chauncey became the first president of the Educational Testing Service, which began administering the SAT widely.

As Lemann reminds us in this important volume, critics emerged early on who worried that the SAT would wind up reducing access to college for people from disadvantaged backgrounds. An early critique came in 1948 from University of Chicago faculty members W. Allison Davis and Robert Havighurst. Davis, perhaps the country's leading Black scholar, and Havighurst believed any form of IQ test rewarded social inheritance rather than measuring potential ability. For them race, socioeconomic status, and other social markers underpredicted the abilities of students from disadvantaged backgrounds on such tests, making the tests suspect.

Conant and Chauncey's vision and Davis and Havighurst's worries have animated the debate over high-stakes testing ever since. Some studies have repeatedly shown that standardized tests do not predict later success and only partially correlate with first-semester grades in college.[2] Even a combination of test scores and grade point averages (GPA) functions as an imperfect predictor of anything more than first-semester grades.[3] For a wide swath of the college-going population, they do not predict if a student will finish their course of study, graduate, and become a leader in their field or society more generally. Yet, as we witnessed in the recent Supreme Court cases on the use of race as one variable in the admissions process at selective colleges and universities, performance on one of the sanctioned college admissions tests (SAT or ACT, which stands for American College Testing, the SAT's rival) factors mightily in how many think about merit.

Recent studies by Raj Chetty and colleagues confirm what many have long argued: performance on such tests is heavily influenced by socioeconomic status. Students from higher socioeconomic groups, irrespective of race, tend to fare better on the exams than students from lower socioeconomic groups.[4] Several factors contribute to this pattern. Typically, more affluent families send their children to schools with greater educational resources—be they public or private. In addition, such families can afford the extra coaching high-achieving students often receive in advance of the testing. Finally, success on the test is openly valued in the family, in the surrounding community, and among one's peers and friends.

Nor is race, regardless of class, an insignificant consideration when we chronicle the history of a test that became *the test*. Experimental social psychologist Claude Steele and students have produced and reproduced several studies that show you can lower performance on standardized tests by inserting key prompts before the test.[5] Tell a Black or female student that they are representing not only themselves but their race or gender, and scores drop for individuals in each group who either are told or believe they are shouldering an individual or collective burden or responsibility. Steele sketches the effects quite beautifully in *Whistling Vivaldi*.

Trying to separate the psychocultural practices of test taking from effects on the tests means that an overreliance on one score, on one day, may result in the unwanted exclusion of talent. As Lemann notes, colleges and universities have sought to adjust for the possibility that they have unfairly diminished the pool by asserting that they seek to capture the total student. This has meant they scrutinize letters of recommendation, extracurricular activities, personal essays, and more.

In another book in the Our Compelling Interests series, *The Walls around Opportunity*, educational scholar Gary Orfield examines the interlacing of housing patterns, state and federal policy, demographic trajectories, and the failure of a color-blind approach in a racially stratified world. These factors produce obstacles to success, which Orfield labels the walls around opportunity in the United States. One of these walls, he maintains, is the wall around admissions to select colleges and universities, which returns us to the role and place of tests and testing.[6] Unquestionably, schools are differentially resourced across the nation. This means colleges and universities have long needed ways of determining whether a grade at one school was equivalent to a grade at another school. Since the advent of mass admissions testing in the 1940s, first the SAT and later the ACT have served as such equalizers, purporting to standardize what we can determine about what students know and can demonstrate.

But the questions of sorting and testing have assumed even more political ballast in a world defined by ever-increasing racial and ethnic diversity. As William Frey noted in the series' inaugural volume, we are on the verge of a diversity explosion.[7] He and other demographers predict a nonwhite majority in the United States by 2040. This demographic transformation is coming just as the numbers of traditional college-age students in the United States continue to decline. This means that while the numbers of absolute college seats exceed seat holders, competition for seats at the most select colleges continues to expand. For modestly endowed, less well-known institutions, these are perilous times. Many have closed and more will close before midcentury.[8] On the other end of the higher education dumbbell sit the schools for whom the SAT and ACT (which was originally meant to be a placement test but has become an admissions test) were designed. Although they form a small fraction of the 4,500-plus postsecondary schools in the United States, they play an outsize role in the public policy debates over race and opportunity and in the ways that many think about the successes and failures of higher education in the United States.

Notwithstanding the hundred or so tests school-age children take before graduating high school today, mass testing of children was not a mainstay when the SAT was created. After the Second World War, President Harry S. Truman formed a president's commission to chart a future for American higher education. After deliberating for over a year, the commission issued its report in 1947.[9] The Truman Commission recommended the democratization of access to college. It called for a massive financial aid program at the undergraduate and graduate levels, free tuition for those attending two-year schools, and a program of continuing education, and it conveyed the sense that education was neither purely utilitarian nor vocational. Reflecting a postwar ethos still being formulated, the commission, over some opposition, called for the end of segregation in the South and the ubiquitous use of quotas against Jews. Coming out of the war, the sentiment emerged that education would be the key to future progress and development and that access to such education needed to be widely available.

In time a tension emerged, one that moved standardized testing from the margins to the center. While the Truman Commission envisioned a democratized educational system open to all, others came to value and champion a select number of private and public institutions that would nurture a kind of talented elite. Most open-access institutions would not need a selection test. Anyone who applied got in. In states with growing populations, such as California, old methods no longer worked after the war. Certifying public high schools had long been a practice before the war in states like Michigan, where the University of Michigan had sent its faculty to certify school curricula as early as 1870. Students who passed a designated, certified curriculum gained admission. California came to adopt an education master plan, crafted by Clark Kerr, president of the University of California system, that directed students through one of three postsecondary doors—community college, a California State university campus, or a campus of the growing University of California system.[10] In the last instance, a validated standardized test became a part of the admissions process.

Testing to control access grew in parallel with the divisions in postwar America. Tests that initially were used to expand the range of students admitted came to be associated with narrowing the range of students admitted. At one level it became a case of supply and demand: there were more applicants to some schools than available seats in the freshman class. At another level it is a story about the testing industry and the underlying paradigm that has prevailed for three-quarters of a century. Starting with Conant and Chauncey, the emphasis was testing for access rather than testing for success beyond first-year academic performance in college. If English is a second or third language for the test taker, what is the conventional admissions test measuring? What if we introduced a series of formative tests for applicants in their first year and allow those who master a subject area to go on?

A useful example may be drawn from the Meyerhoff Scholars Program, crafted by Freeman Hrabowski and the University of Maryland, Baltimore County. Hrabowski and colleagues learned that students in STEM (science, technology, engineering, and mathematics) fields graduated at higher levels if they got at least a B in introductory calculus and a couple of other core classes.[11] Rather than selecting students for prior preparation, they modified the curriculum to allow students to repeat core introductory courses until they could show the needed mastery. This redesign amounted to a testing regimen for success and not just access.

The recent Supreme Court decision ending the use of race as a variable in the admissions process will undoubtedly drive new policies and innovations. As Lemann speculates, it could result in some schools abandoning admissions tests altogether. In recent years the test-optional movement has gained momentum across the United States, especially among elite liberal arts schools with national reputations. That movement raises the possibility that a class can be constructed without an overreliance on standardized tests. This prompts the question of how we have identified and defined merit and how we should henceforth.

Key to identifying the next steps to be taken is an understanding of the demographic reality pinpointed in the first volume in the Our Compelling Interests series and in Orfield's volume *The Walls around Opportunity*. As Lemann notes, when the California Master Plan was introduced, the population across the state was 92 percent white; it is now 35 percent white. Orfield found that Black and Brown students account for the majority of public school students, yet the University of California system is nearly two-fifths white and one-third Asian.[12] The passage of Proposition 209, which banned the use of race in the admissions process long before the recent Supreme Court decision, foretold what would happen to the makeup of elite campuses: except for a rise in the percentage of Asians, they would look more like they did in the 1960s—at least for a while.[13] Some may believe that going backward is going forward but does doing so allow us to value and leverage diversity for the benefit of the nation and our democracy?

But as Patricia Gándara notes in her comment, the removal of test scores as a factor in the admissions process has been liberatory for Black and Brown students in California.

Gándara was a member of a task force assigned to evaluate the continued use of SAT or ACT scores for admission into the University of California system of schools. Subsequently, the regents of the University of California recommended the abandonment of test scores and the use of thirteen other factors in the admissions process. The result was a surge of Black and Brown applicants and a noticeable increase in their presence on University of California campuses. She writes that after the decision to drop the SAT by the University of California Board of Regents, "Black freshman applicants rose by about 48 percent at both the University of California, Los Angeles, and the University of California, Berkeley, and Latino applicants increased by 33 percent at UCLA and 36 percent at Berkeley. This resulted in historically high rates of admission for these groups." By the summer of 2023, while 40 percent of the state's population, Latinos represented 22.5 percent of University of California students; Blacks, 6.5 percent of the overall state population, accounted for 5.5 percent of the University of California undergraduate population.

Looking ahead, we are left to ask, is diversity still a compelling state interest? Was the concern for generating a racially and ethnically diverse class at selective institutions a corollary to Conant and Chauncey's desire to seed a meritorious elite? While rejecting one dimension of the diversity argument that has guided policy since the 1978 *Bakke* decision, the Supreme Court did not reject diversity as a compelling interest entirely. It carved out a special provision for the military academies to continue to identify and select recruits from all parts of the nation and to use race as a variable in the crafting of a class. Critics on the right complain that this is a zero-sum proposition. Race should never be a factor in admissions, even if there is a reason to believe it brings value.[14]

At some level the Court acknowledged what Scott Page argues in his book in our series *The Diversity Bonus*. According to Page, there are times when diversity matters less. If you need a lumberjack, he believes, you select the most capable, fittest lumberjack. But in a knowledge economy, where problems are often complex, research shows you gain a bonus when assigning a diverse set of actors to solving the problem. In such instances, an assembly of the smartest people from the same schools with similar backgrounds doesn't produce the breakthroughs needed.[15] The Court implicitly acknowledged that warfare and military strategy may benefit from pulling together a range of appropriately educated individuals and that the academies needed to generate that leadership. The decision seems to suggest diversity in the military would also contribute to group unity in the field.

Left unaddressed by the Court, however, is the question posed by Lemann and further considered by Marvin Krislov in his commentary. Tests have been used as a proxy for merit. They have been believed to be a good predictor of academic success, as a recent commentary in the *New York Times* by columnist David Leonhardt argues,[16] although studies have long shown that they better approximate first-semester college GPA than they predict leadership, creativity, or other markers of a successful collegiate experience. But as Krislov notes, they also track with socioeconomic background, blurring the lines between meritocracy and aristocracy.

This book, and the series of which it is a part, assumes that talent is distributed across the nation and world but access to opportunity is not. It invites the reader to understand the history of standardized testing and the creation of a testing industry that began with hopes of expanding opportunity and democratizing access at elite colleges, and it shows how, rather than shattering class privileges, the exams reinforced the relation between doing well on the tests and coming from families and neighborhoods with considerable resources. At its core the book asks us to think deeply about what is meant by merit. Can one test, taken over a few hours, tell us all we need to know about a potential candidate? It also cautions us that finding suitable alternatives to tests that have been validated over decades may take more than a minute. As important, it invites us to probe our commitment to equal opportunity in the United States by asking, what is the purpose of access to education? This question is always important to revisit. The answers we offer have deep importance in a world shaped by technological change, violent geopolitical conflicts, growing distrust of institutions, and an ever-widening gap between educational achievers and those who never get the chance to show their talents.

CHAPTER 1

The Birth of the
American Meritocracy

IN THE SUMMER OF 1948, Henry Chauncey, the president of
the brand-new Educational Testing Service (ETS), read an article that he found quite disturbing. It was in a journal called the
Scientific Monthly; its title was "The Measurement of Mental
Systems (Can Intelligence Be Measured?)," and its authors were
W. Allison Davis, an anthropologist who was at that moment
possibly the most prominent Black academic in the United
States, and Robert Havighurst, a colleague of Davis's at the University of Chicago. They argued that intelligence tests were a
fraud, a way of wrapping the fortunate children of the middle
and upper classes in a mantle of scientifically demonstrated superiority. The tests, they wrote, measured only "a very narrow
range of mental activities" and carried "a strong cultural handi-
cap for pupils of lower socioeconomic groups." They assessed
"academic or linguistic activities" and then submitted themselves to a kind of circular validation process, because "a teacher's
rating of a pupil is an estimate of the pupil's performance on
the same kind of problems as those in the standard tests."[1]

Chauncey was the scion of a New England Puritan family—he was a direct descendant of Charles Chauncy, the second president of Harvard College—who was born in 1905, the same year that the first intelligence test was administered by Alfred Binet in Paris. As a college freshman he had taken a course on mental tests and become entranced with them, believing them to be a scientific miracle with unlimited potential to better humanity. Although he was one of the founders of what some people now call "meritocracy" in America (the word didn't exist at the time ETS was founded), Chauncey himself had the virtues prized by a previous system of elite selection: he was tall, handsome, athletic, energetic, public spirited, optimistic, and a natural leader, but not especially intellectual. He believed that mental tests were a great technological innovation, like the telephone or the light bulb, and so could only be beneficial, but he didn't have a particular social vision that he wanted tests to serve. He simply believed in them. Indeed, through the years of ETS's greatest growth, driven by its devising and administering aptitude-based tests for admission to selective colleges and universities, Chauncey tried constantly to find other kinds of tests for ETS to offer, mainly without success.

As a young man, Chauncey had become an assistant dean at Harvard, a job that he came to find frustratingly minor. In 1933, he acquired a new boss: James Bryant Conant, a chemist who was Harvard's first non–Boston Brahmin president in more than sixty years. Conant shared Chauncey's interest in testing, but he had far more definite ideas than Chauncey did about what testing's purpose should be. The Harvard College that Conant took over was dominated by boarding school graduates from prosperous families in the Northeast. Its admissions test was a battery of essay exams administered by the College Entrance Examination Board (known as the College Board), then a small organization that had been created in 1900 to align the curricula of a few dozen mostly private schools with a handful of elite private colleges and universities. It was quite difficult for public school students, and students from the middle of the country, even to take these exams let alone to excel on them, not only because of their content but also because the number of test sites was limited.

Conant told Chauncey that he wanted to start a new scholarship program at Harvard, aimed at students who wouldn't ordinarily take the College Board tests. He assigned Chauncey to find a test that was as close as possible to an IQ test—that is, one that measured what Conant saw as innate intellectual ability, unconnected to the quality of the applicant's high school education. After some searching, Chauncey met a Princeton professor named Carl Brigham, who had worked on the first mass administration of an IQ test, to U.S. Army inductees in the First World War, and had gone on to produce an adaptation of that test for college admissions purposes. Brigham called it the Scholastic Aptitude Test. He administered it experimentally for the first time in 1926. And now Harvard adopted it for its new scholarship program.

The new Harvard scholarship program was a great success by Conant's and Chauncey's lights. Soon Harvard was using the SAT as a selection device for all its scholarship students. Then it persuaded all the other College Board schools to use the SAT as their scholarship selection device. During the Second World War, Chauncey supervised the administration of an adapted SAT called the Army-Navy College Qualification Test—used to select soldiers for specialized, technical roles in the service—to more than three hundred thousand high school seniors on a single day. This proved it would be possible for a testing agency to scan an entire age cohort simultaneously, as a prelude to assigning them to the roles for which they were supposedly best suited. Also during the war, the College Board dropped its old essay exams and made the SAT its sole college admissions test. During the years after the war, a series of adept maneuvers by Conant and Chauncey led to the establishment of ETS in Princeton, New Jersey, to maintain the SAT and to develop a broad range of other exams for the College Board and other clients. Chauncey, in becoming ETS's president, was able to take on a role commensurate with his ambitions.

So when he came across the article by Davis and Havighurst, he was annoyed: here was a sentiment that he hadn't encountered during the preceding fifteen years of uninterrupted ascension for the SAT. "They take the extreme and, I believe, radical point of view that any test items showing different difficulties for different socioeconomic groups are inappropriate," Chauncey wrote in a diary that he kept at the time. He continued: "If ability has any relation to success in life parents in upper socio-economic groups should have more ability than those in lower socio-economic groups. And if there is anything in heredity (such as tall parents having tall children) one would expect children of high socio-economic group parents to have more ability than children of low socio-economic group parents."[2]

We are conditioned to think of the moment when Chauncey was writing this entry in his journal—the post–Second World

War moment—as one of a great democratization of higher education, and perhaps of American life generally. The GI Bill opened up to millions of veterans who would not otherwise have gone past high school the possibility of getting college degrees. Their successful experience convinced the country that many more Americans could benefit from higher education, and this conviction underlay a historically unprecedented expansion of American colleges and universities (and, perhaps as a consequence, of the size and well-being of the American middle class). I will go into more detail about this expansion in the next chapter. For now, it's important to keep in mind that Chauncey and Conant's project to establish the SAT as the standard admissions device for higher education was a separate endeavor, though also a highly consequential one. It aimed to change the student population, and by extension the overall nature, of a limited number of highly selective colleges and universities. It was driven by a vision of the American future, but we should be precise about what that vision was: a more democratically selected educated elite, not greatly enhanced opportunity for the majority of Americans, and not the advancement of historically marginalized people. A great deal of trouble has come from our tendency to conflate elite selection with mass opportunity. My aim in this chapter is to disentangle them. That is a necessary precondition to thinking clearly about testing.

Chauncey, whom I got to know well in the final years of his very long life (he died in 2002, a few weeks short of his ninety-eighth birthday), would have been amazed, at least back in 1948, to learn that the objections Davis and Havighurst were raising would one day become widespread and potent, so much so as to threaten the SAT existentially. How could he have failed to see this? He and his colleagues inhabited a small, tightly enclosed world—Chauncey and many of his close friends and professional associates were fellow graduates of a single small New England boarding school, Groton—in which everything implied by the terms "diversity," "equity," and "inclusion," which educators use constantly today, simply wasn't part of the conversation. The moral wrong represented by the pervasive American system of racial rank ordering—calling attention to which was the central theme of Davis's career—was strikingly absent from the consciousness of most of America's elite white liberals, even at a time when the early stirrings of the civil rights movement should have been clearly visible to them. During the early years of ETS, the global competition between the United States and the Soviet Union was the overwhelming preoccupation of the American establishment, and most of its members believed that the central task of educators should be to play their part in this struggle.

That isn't to say the SAT did not have a social vision behind it, as all widely used tests must. That vision, powerfully motivating in the minds of its early champions, is so different from the way admissions tests function now, and from the grounds on which they are defended, that it requires explanation.

Carl Brigham, the SAT's inventor, was as a young man an enthusiastic member of the eugenics movement—which, in the early twentieth century, captured the imagination of much of the American patrician class with its lurid warnings about the country's being overwhelmed by high-breeding, genetically inferior members of the lower orders. The eugenicists were definitely racists, though the primary targets of their racism were people who would now be considered white, like Catholics and Jews who had recently come to the United States from southern and eastern Europe. Brigham wrote a book based on the results of the U.S. Army intelligence tests, called *A Study of American Intelligence*, affirming these prejudices. "American intelligence is declining, and will proceed with an accelerating rate as the racial admixture becomes more and more extensive," he wrote. "These are the plain, if somewhat ugly, facts that our study shows."[3]

But, almost alone among prominent eugenicists, Brigham had a change of heart. In 1928, only two years after the debut of the SAT, he renounced his former views publicly at a convention of eugenicists, and in 1930 he issued a formal retraction of *A Study of American Intelligence*, calling it "pretentious" and "without foundation."[4] In 1932 he published a book pointedly titled *A Study of Error*. In 1935, in an unpublished manuscript, Brigham wrote, "The test movement came into this country some twenty-five or thirty years ago accompanied by one of the most glorious fallacies in the history of science, namely, that the tests measured *native intelligence* purely and simply without regard to training or schooling. I hope nobody believes that now. The test scores definitely are a composite including schooling, family background, familiarity with English, and everything else, relevant and irrelevant. The '*native intelligence*' hypothesis is dead."

One of Brigham's complaints was that the people conducting research on intelligence testing were the same people who were promoting the idea of native intelligence as a single, all-important inherited trait. They assumed that test results measured an immutable property of the brain, and their research always confirmed their theory. The most important of these promoters was Lewis Terman, a Stanford professor who had adapted Binet's test for American use and who devised the ubiquitous concept of IQ, or intelligence quotient. Binet had developed his test to identify children who might need special help as they entered France's newly universal public elementary school system, so that they could succeed there. Terman had an opposite concern, with identifying young people whose scores were unusually high so that they could develop their talents through special educational opportunities. His main concern about students other than the highest scorers was that they would hold back the super-brainy by being put in classes alongside them. The formerly widespread use of IQ test–based tracking systems in American public schools owed a lot to Terman's influence.

Conant, from what we know, was not a eugenicist, but he was a believer in Terman's ideas about what IQ tests measured and the uses to which their results should be put. During and after his twenty-year reign as president of Harvard, he exercised a broad national influence beyond what any one university president does today; he played a large part not only in the rise of the SAT but also in the development of the atomic bomb, the creation of the National Science Foundation, and many other initiatives. So while his interest in the SAT began as part of a crusade to remake the student body of Harvard College, it quickly became part of a much larger project. Conant wanted to remake American society as a whole, and it wasn't implausible for him to believe he could have a significant influence there.

In a series of writings during the Second World War, Conant laid out his ideas. He had two main concerns: that the country's vast, decentralized public school system would permit the talents of potential top scientists and technocrats to go undetected and therefore unused in the great struggles of the postwar era; and that America would develop debilitating class tensions that would leave it unable to compete successfully with rivals who claimed to have classless societies. Conant certainly hadn't dropped his concern with the composition of the student body of the university he led, but he was not, as so many people are now, primarily concerned with making admissions a fair contest so that precious slots in the Harvard student body would go to the people who most deserved them. (And anyway, Harvard at the time accepted two-thirds of its applicants.) His sights were set higher than that. In an article in the *Atlantic Monthly* in 1943 titled "Wanted: American Radicals," Conant called for the creation of a new ideal American type, a kind of frontiersman of the modern age,[5] who would be "a fanatical believer in equality," committed to "wielding the axe against the root of inherited privilege."[6] What this hotblooded rhetoric obscures is that Conant's aim was to confer large opportunities on a small group of people; the devotion to equality and hatred of privilege he envisioned pertained to the selection method, not the overall character of American society.

From the vantage point of today, it's hard to imagine how Conant could have believed that instantiating the SAT as one of society's basic sorting mechanisms would lead to this kind of result. It helps explain his thinking to understand that he assumed the SAT did not measure education, family background, or preparation, only innate mental ability. Therefore it would be class neutral because—another of Conant's assumptions—the highest scorers would be scattered almost randomly around the country. Conant further assumed that whatever opportunity a very high SAT score opened up for somebody, it would not be heritable: on the model of those chosen to be guardians in Plato's imaginary republic, that person's children would return to the ranks of ordinary people. Unlike members of anointed elite groups in the past, they would not try to turn themselves into a hereditary aristocracy. (In his article, Conant proposed that all personal wealth be legally confiscated at death.) Conant, who had Europe's elite universities in mind as a model, thought of the SAT as a device to select people for roles that were important but not especially remunerative. Those who got high scores and were tracked for special roles would become, essentially, public servants, working for large government agencies or universities, indifferent to money and status.

To clarify Conant's very non-twenty-first-century idea of what constituted a radically democratized United States, it may help to consider three public campaigns he waged in the years after the war: against the GI Bill; in favor of mandatory universal national service; and in favor of the creation of large comprehensive public high schools in the burgeoning suburbs. What tied these together was Conant's fervent belief in elite selection, combined with his equally fervent belief in national cohesion. National service and public school were meant to bring all Americans together into a shared, government-managed, character-shaping experience while they were young. But this would happen before they arrived in the higher education system, which Conant believed should be an experience for the few—the right few—and not the many. Along with other prominent presidents of private universities (Robert Maynard Hutchins of the University of Chicago wrote an article about the GI Bill called "The Threat to American Education"), he was actively opposed to the great historic expansion of higher education after the war.

Chauncey was always loyal to Conant, his patron. When a Boston newspaper criticized Conant for his opposition to the GI Bill, Chauncey fired off a letter to the editor insisting that expanding access to higher education was not related to his and Conant's notion of what enhanced educational opportunity in the postwar era would mean. He wrote,

> Equality of opportunity in the early days of our country did not mean that every boy became president of a bank, a railroad magnate or the captain of a ship. But each boy did have the opportunity to rise to such positions if his talent and industry qualified him.
>
> Today the lower rungs of the ladder are educational. Climbing these rungs involves the same competitive element entailed a century ago by the ladder of opportunity.[7]

But Chauncey's own preoccupations during those years were not exactly the same as Conant's. Foremost was his interest in building ETS into a large, important organization. Chauncey did this amazingly well; ETS's ascent was steep and largely uninterrupted up to his retirement in 1970. ETS as an organization was a major beneficiary of the development that Conant had opposed: the building of the world's first mass higher education system in the postwar United States. ETS and the College Board had a sales force that traveled the country persuading colleges and universities to join the College

Board, which also meant adopting the SAT. The College Board's membership grew from dozens to thousands, and the annual number of SAT test takers grew from thousands to millions. The system was financed through fees paid by test takers, so, for a college or university, requiring the SAT of applicants increased the income of ETS and the College Board without incurring any direct cost.

Unlike Conant, Chauncey was enthusiastic about all testing, not intelligence testing in particular. During the early years of ETS, he devoted a great deal of energy to promoting an idea he called the Census of Abilities: a battery of tests that would measure every significant human trait, including, for example, persistence and sense of humor. Every young American would be measured by these as yet unwritten tests and then matched with the most appropriate destiny based on the results. It's worth bearing in mind that the country had a far more top-down official culture back then, which accorded authority figures an automatic respect that is almost unimaginable today. Students were not told their SAT scores until the late 1950s; it was assumed that they would gratefully accept the advice of their guidance counselors about what college to aim for. Chauncey assumed that the results of other life-shaping tests would be received with similar passive gratitude. He attempted to make ETS the purveyor of many different kinds of tests, including personality tests like the popular Myers-Briggs Type Indicator, which was initially developed at ETS. He pitched his big idea in many high places, including, briefly, the Truman White House. But during his time at the helm of ETS, nothing ever worked out except for admissions tests for higher education. Chauncey was left proselytizing for just a portion of the testing regime he dreamed of, though that didn't diminish his energetic enthusiasm.

By the time Chauncey retired from ETS, the mature testing system that he, Conant, and others had built may bring to mind the fable of the blind men and the elephant: the system was pervasive and consequential, and every group that played a part in it believed it had hold of something different. Chauncey and many of his colleagues at ETS thought they were operating a benign, paternalistic, scientifically advanced national personnel office that would direct appreciative young people to the roles that would make them happiest and would best serve the needs of society. Conant believed he was creating a new elite of technocratic public servants who would steer the country successfully through the Cold War and orient the leading universities toward high-level scientific research. The mass of colleges and universities that began using admissions tests believed they were modernizing and enhancing their prestige by associating themselves with the norms and practices of the leading institutions in their field. And many students and their families regarded the system as an important means of allocating a scarce and valuable resource—tickets to success in America. So their relationship to testing and admissions was anything but passive; by the late 1950s, commercial test preparation, which ETS and the College Board insisted was a fraud, was a small industry on its way to becoming a much larger one.

And the concern that Davis and Havighurst had expressed, presciently, in 1948—that widespread admissions testing using adapted IQ tests would serve to reinforce, not overturn, existing systems of social advantage—became far more widespread.

In general, test scores do not, as Conant predicted, destroy inherited privilege; they reflect it—there are substantial score gaps, on average, by race and class. Indeed, it is possible to produce a neo-eugenicist work like Richard Herrnstein and Charles Murray's *The Bell Curve* (1994) by using SAT score data as the assumed measure of innate, substantially inherited native intelligence and then treating the score gaps as evidence of the presence of genetically ordained differences in intelligence between Blacks and whites. Because of the racial gaps in scores, the pervasiveness of testing forced selective colleges and universities that wanted to become more racially integrated to set aside a strict adherence to test scores as an admissions device. That, in turn, triggered a long series of lawsuits and state ballot initiatives launched by mainly white opponents of affirmative action policies, who charged, using test scores as their evidence, that they were being discriminated against in admissions. (I will discuss this in more detail in chapter 3.) There may be no issue on which the Supreme Court, through more than half a dozen cases stretching over half a century, has sent a less clear signal than on the question of whether it's okay to privilege achieving a racially integrated student body over adhering to test scores as a primary admissions device. With the passage of time, the controversies over admissions testing seem to have become more intense, not less. The tests represent a social order founded outside the usual processes of democratic consultation, which has had trouble withstanding the stresses of public life.

By the time the Supreme Court, in June 2023, had ruled that race-conscious affirmative action programs in higher education are unconstitutional, more than 1,500 colleges and universities had already adopted test-optional policies for their applicants, partly because of the COVID-19 pandemic and partly in anticipation of the Court's decision. The University of California had banned the use of admissions tests entirely. ETS and the College Board have moved beyond their long-standing economic dependence on IQ-descended college admissions tests. In the wake of the Supreme Court decision and the end of the pandemic, several highly selective universities—at this writing, Brown, Dartmouth, Harvard, MIT, the University of Texas at Austin, and Yale—have announced the resumption of SAT requirements for all their applicants. Most others have not. It seems possible that the Court's decision will lead some universities to affirm their use of admissions tests, but most to deemphasize or drop testing. It feels as if a seventy-five-year era—the era of aptitude-based testing as an admissions device—may now be coming to an end, substantially because of the stark conflict between the rhetoric of democratic promise that ushered in the era and the quite different effect it has had in practice. Now it's time to think about what form the next era should take, and what role testing should play in it.

CHAPTER 2

Higher Education
for All

THE GI BILL was signed into law in 1944. In 1946, Harry
Truman appointed the President's Commission on Higher
Education, led by George F. Zook, the president of the American Council on Education—a Kansas farm boy who went on
to become a historian, president of the University of Akron,
and U.S. commissioner of education. The commission worked
quickly and issued a five-volume report at the end of 1947.

The Truman Commission report makes for a striking contrast with the writings of James Bryant Conant and Henry
Chauncey at roughly the same time. Its focus was overwhelmingly on expanding access to higher education—it called for
making the GI Bill a permanent policy, rather than a one-time
benefit for veterans. The commission recommended that the
federal government put $120 million a year into financial aid
for students who couldn't otherwise afford to go to college
and that it create another new program that would pay for
thirty thousand students a year to go to graduate school. All
Americans, the commission said, should finish high school

and go on to two years of college, tuition-free. Tuition for the last two years of college should be reduced to where it had been ten years earlier. For older Americans, the universities should undertake a major new program of adult education, funded by the federal government. And this expanded higher education system should not be entirely vocational. For example, the report said, "farmers need the satisfactions that come from literature, music, painting, and philosophy as well as those to be derived from material goods."[1]

The report was almost entirely concerned with public higher education, so much so that two members of the commission who worked at private universities filed a dissent saying that institutions like theirs should get federal funds too. It had essentially nothing to say about admissions, surely because the part of the higher education system it was focused on expanding was not selective. It actively dismissed the idea that only a limited number of Americans were smart enough to benefit from a college education: "The Commission does not subscribe to the belief that higher education should be confined to an intellectual elite, much less a smaller elite drawn largely from families in the higher income brackets."[2] And, years in advance of the Supreme Court's ruling that racial segregation in public schools was unconstitutional, it called for an immediate end to segregation in colleges and universities in the South, for an end to the common practice of quotas limiting the number of Jewish students, and for an end to "antifeminism in higher education." The commission's four Southern members refused to endorse its recommendation that racial segregation be ended.

The commission's most striking recommendations were of course never enacted, and indeed they still seem radical all these years later. While the commission was doing its work, a backstage drama was taking place that concerned who would be in charge of the admissions testing regime that Conant and Chauncey wanted to institute. Zook thought it should be an American Council on Education project, in light of the council's eminence in the education world. The Carnegie Corporation, an ally of Conant's presided over by a fellow graduate of Groton and Harvard, intervened: it made a $50,000 grant to the council, and Zook stood down. The College Board also had to be subjected to some combination of persuasion and muscle to agree to the establishment of ETS to produce and administer multiple-choice, IQ-like admissions tests on its behalf. It mattered, too, that Carl Brigham, the inventor of the SAT, who had developed grave doubts about its widespread use, had died in 1943, at the age of fifty-three. In the end the significant opposition was quelled and, just one week after the Truman Commission issued its report, ETS was officially chartered.

The U.S. Constitution does not mention education, but the country was nonetheless early in establishing free public education. By the late nineteenth century, a large majority of American children were being educated at public expense through the eighth grade, which put the United States well ahead of the rest of the world as a universal educator. Although the advent of free public school had notable champions, like Horace Mann, it is better understood as the product of a slowly emerging national consensus than of a single policy decision. It was carried out by state governments and by thousands of local school boards. This meant that, as is eternally the case in most areas of American education, a number of quite different rationales for expansion were operating at the same time. Schools would create good citizens and make our democracy function better. Schools would put students on the road to individual success. Schools would promote local economic development. Schools would teach children to question authority. Schools would teach children to obey authority. The lack of clarity about its purpose probably helped public education's expansion, while also guaranteeing that it would generate perpetual disputes.

In 1900, only a little over 3 percent of American public school students were enrolled in high school. There were only ninety-five thousand high school graduates in the country, out of a national population of seventy-six million. (It took until the middle of the twentieth century for most American teenagers to be enrolled in high school, and until decades after that for a majority to graduate.) Fewer than two hundred thousand students were enrolled in college in 1900—just over 2 percent of the college-age population. It's understandable that at the time when the College Board was established, the project of selecting which lucky few people among a great mass of applicants should be admitted to college was not on anybody's mind. Even the most established colleges were only minimally selective; until 1920, the Ivy League schools had a policy of accepting all applicants they deemed academically qualified. (It's still the case today, of course, that the vast majority of American colleges are only minimally selective.)

In the early years of college admissions and admissions testing,[3] the main goal of the colleges was to exert some influence on what was taught in high schools, partly out of a sense of civic responsibility and partly as a way of ensuring that incoming students would be well prepared. High schools, for their part, were interested in sparing themselves and their students the trouble of negotiating a different set of entrance requirements for each college. Because the extreme decentralization of American education made it almost insuperably difficult to impose realistic uniform requirements on all applicants nationwide, any early democratizing impulse the colleges might have had inevitably meant loosening their admissions regimes to some extent. The College Board grew out of an initiative called the Committee of Ten, chaired by Harvard's president, Charles William Eliot, which issued a report in 1892 whose most daring recommendation was that the required number of high school courses in Greek for applicants to elite colleges be lowered from three to two. The College Board itself, which now seems to have been impossibly narrow and non-inclusive at its founding, was meant to make its member colleges just a little more broadly accessible across a narrow range of high schools, and most of its higher education members initially continued to offer their own entrance exams as an alternative to the College Board's.

It was common for state universities to "certify" public high schools—that is, to act as a kind of accrediting body. Then any graduate of a certified high school in the state would be automatically admitted to the university. The University of Michigan launched a certification system in 1870, having abandoned an earlier system in which it operated high schools of its own. (Graduates of noncertified Michigan high schools would have to take a university-specific entrance exam.) Michigan faculty members would make annual inspection visits to the certified schools, to ensure that they were offering genuine college preparatory work. In this way the state universities and their faculties were actively involved in improving and standardizing high school education. This was not an entirely idealistic project. There was an element of elitism, because only the strongest high schools were certified, and of self-interest, because the universities, struggling to establish themselves, were getting a reliable supply of students. Another common admissions practice was "conditioned" admittance, in which a student who had not completed the entrance requirements or passed the exams could enroll anyway and use good academic performance in college as a substitute for the usual admission standards. This too was in the economic interest of colleges, because it increased their student population. Or, less formally, a college could simply admit all comers and see who made it all the way through to graduation.

As it had with elementary and secondary education, the United States during the nineteenth century began to develop a higher education system that was far more widely accessible than any other country's. To the extent that there was a legislative landmark that established this as a national policy, it was the passage in 1862 of the Morrill Act, which offered states free federal land if they would create colleges that taught "agriculture and the mechanic arts." The law's author, Congressman Justin Morrill, a blacksmith's son from Vermont, said he intended for these colleges to be "accessible to all, but especially to the sons of toil."[4] The Morrill Act led directly to the establishment of such major institutions as Cornell University and the University of California, but states had already been creating public universities for decades. These were generally almost or completely tuition-free, open to all, and focused on instruction in practical and useful subjects that would lead directly to a livelihood, rather than on the classical education that the older, private universities were offering. The states also established "normal schools," which trained mostly female students to become public school teachers. Community colleges (originally called junior colleges), which represent a newer and even broader tradition in American higher education, expanded tremendously during the twentieth century, from one institution in 1901 to more than 1,200, with more than four million students, by 1980. (There are more than eight million community college students today.) More than 40 percent of American undergraduates, and most undergraduates of color, are enrolled at community colleges.

Like the elementary and secondary schools, but perhaps even more so, America's colleges and universities in the aggregate represented a messy mixture of different purposes and rationales. Often this mixture could be found in synecdoche form inside a single institution. Most of the country's private institutions of higher education had their roots in religion, and still had strong religious elements through at least the end of the nineteenth century. Back then, the private institutions were also likely to place a heavy emphasis on Greek and Latin. The prosperity of the Gilded Age turned the Ivy League, and to some extent the flagship state universities and many private liberal arts colleges as well, into playgrounds for hard-partying children of the prosperous classes. College athletics was becoming a national preoccupation. And outside the most prestigious private institutions, the country had developed separate, unequal higher education systems for Blacks and women.

Business tycoons, especially if they were self-made, routinely told the public that they considered higher education to be useless or counterproductive. Lawrence Vesey's *The Emergence of the American University* reproduces this quote from Andrew Carnegie in 1889: "While the college student has been learning a little about the barbarous and petty squabbles of a far-distant past, or trying to master languages which are dead, such knowledge as seems adapted for life upon another planet than this as far as business affairs are concerned, the future captain of industry is hotly engaged in the school of experience, obtaining the very knowledge required for his future triumphs. . . . College education as it exists is fatal to success in that domain."[5]

But Carnegie, and many of his fellow robber barons, were soon to become major donors to universities, and universities were putting a great deal of effort into courting their largesse. The public universities, especially, were aligning themselves with local commercial interests, launching academic programs meant to supply employers skilled workers and to provide the children of farmers and other workers with the opportunity to join the middle class via utilitarian instruction. From the point of view of senior administrators and faculty members, by far the most important development in university-based higher education was the spreading embrace of the research university model, featuring the establishment of powerful disciplinary organizations, doctoral programs, academic tenure, and the idea that professors had a dual mission of teaching and research, with research in the position of primary importance.

The advent of significant federal research funding after the Second World War made becoming a leading research university an especially attractive prospect.

The adoption of the SAT, though exciting to its small number of promoters and alarming to its even smaller number of critics, understandably did not stand out as a signal development in American higher education and American society until years later. Before the Second World War, the question of who would be admitted to a selective college or professional school and who would be rejected had not risen to the level of clear national importance, if for no other reasons than that relatively few Americans went to college and the colleges they attended, even elite ones, were, by today's standards, close to being open access. IQ and IQ-related testing still had the sheen of newness—even of being a liberal enthusiasm, with only a handful of dissenters like Brigham and W. Allison Davis.

In 1951, the American Council on Education published an eight-hundred-page volume called *Educational Measurement*, organized by Zook, the former chairman of the Truman Commission, and edited by E. F. Lindquist of the University of Iowa, who was widely considered to be the country's leading psychometrician. The book is mainly focused on testing in higher education, or between high school and college. Much of it is technical. But it's striking, as the Truman Commission report is, for the difference of its concerns from Conant's. It mentions the SAT and aptitude testing only in passing, even though one of the contributors was Chauncey, writing in partnership with one of his colleagues at ETS; in fact it hardly mentions the use of testing as an admissions selection device.

Its overwhelming concern is with using testing to create an individually tailored system of instruction that will help each student succeed in higher education. The book is especially skeptical of ability grouping. "The first consideration is that students should be classified in such a way that no embarrassment or stigma is attached," the introductory essay says. And a few pages later, the authors observe, "The goal here is . . . to discover effective methods of providing for individual needs and capacities. . . . Measurement has an important role in the process." Later they note, "Too frequently the emphasis is placed on discovering pupils who cannot profit from a given course of instruction rather than on determining the optimum course for each pupil."[6]

One member of the advisory committee Zook put together to oversee the book was Ben D. Wood of Columbia University's Teachers College. Wood, a brilliant, eccentric, opinionated man who is generally considered to be the inventor of the multiple-choice test, had helped supervise a long-running study of public education in Pennsylvania during the 1930s. From that he concluded—as his coauthor, William Learned, had concluded in a major earlier study—that schools at all levels were granting credits and degrees to students essentially on the basis of their presence, without bothering to find out whether they had learned anything. (Wood himself had been essentially home-schooled, or self-educated, during a childhood spent on a remote ranch in Texas and didn't feel he was any the worse for it.) One can feel Wood's intellectual presence throughout the book, and with it an idealistic early-stage vision of standardized testing as a means for educating more people more fully, by finding out how much material they had truly mastered and then tailoring their placement, counseling, and instruction so as to maximize their chances of mastering more material. Testing would serve the goal of widespread learning, on the assumption that every student could learn. It would make educational opportunity more widespread, not more restricted.

Why didn't this dream come true? Reimagining standardized testing as a project whose aim was to promote more widespread, meaningful learning, rather than selection, would have been expensive, just as enacting the full recommendations of the Truman Commission report would have been. It would have imposed some degree of external control on an educational system presided over mainly by states and local communities, and so would have been unpopular with many stakeholders. It would have implied a major reorientation of public higher education toward teaching, counseling, and guidance—another expensive commitment for a system that was being nearly overwhelmed by new students, and one that didn't represent what many professors and administrators wanted. More broadly, ideas about testing are expressions of ideas about American society. The years after the Second World War demonstrated the limits of New Deal liberalism, absent the immediate threats of economic depression and war; Truman-era dreams about expanded health care and other aspects of the welfare state also failed to materialize. The rising claims of previously excluded groups generated a backlash against generous, inclusive social policies. And in the later decades of the twentieth century, the rise of neoliberalism led to a redefinition of standardized testing as a means of outside evaluation of educators' performance, and of the redirection of education's purpose toward economic utility.

In an ideal world, what would have happened during the last half of the twentieth century is something more in the spirit of the Truman Commission report: a far greater emphasis on access and affordability in the expansion of higher education, and the use of testing mainly as a diagnostic tool that would help colleges and universities create more widespread academic success, culminating in degree completion, for their students. Instead, the country pursued a profoundly mixed course. Higher education expanded dramatically, from just over two million students, in fewer than 2,000 institutions, in 1950 to more than fourteen million students, in more than 3,500 institutions, in 1990; today, more than 90 percent of young Americans have at least some interaction with higher education. The association between degrees in higher education and socioeconomic status rose significantly. But the prestige and the convenience of aptitude-based testing for selection caused it to spread in the postwar decades to a far greater extent than did testing regimes based on different educational visions. Testing, universal higher education, and inequality (among educational institutions and among their graduates individually) all increased together.

The result was a system that, at its best, can provide genuine educational opportunities to people from all backgrounds but that on the whole performs far better for the already fortunate. The gap in college accessibility between children of high-status families and children of low-status families has widened. The association between an education that ends with high school education and adult prosperity has decreased. Voices that were generally not heard in education policy debates in the mid-twentieth century and before—students, people of color—have begun to make themselves consequential, and they often have strong objections to the testing system. We do not have the kind of widely accessible and effective democratic education system that public-sector leaders like Zook dreamed of creating. Something closer to Conant's vision, of an education and testing system built around elite selection, came to pass, but without generating the spirit of national cohesion that he had in mind.

One might wonder whether the two visions of American higher education in the second half of the twentieth century—one universalizing, one selection oriented, each served by tests of different kinds—could have been combined. The person who most stands out for having tried to do that in a systematic way is Clark Kerr, who served as chancellor of the University of California, Berkeley, and then president of the University of California during the 1950s and 1960s. Now largely forgotten, he was the most celebrated and influential American in higher education of his era, and a man whose successes and failures are still instructive. Kerr, a labor economist who had grown up in a devout Quaker family on a farm in eastern Pennsylvania, was an extremely precise and organized man who had the good luck to preside over the country's premier state higher education system at a time when it, like California, was prosperous and growing. He believed in both the democratic promise of higher education and the importance of protecting the high end of the system from democratizing impulses. To his mind these were not inconsistent beliefs, though combining them seamlessly was challenging. The immediate bureaucratic and political problem that concerned him was that California's state colleges, which had mostly begun as normal schools and were ambitious in ways that are typical of institutions, wanted to be able to confer doctoral degrees. Kerr felt this would threaten the excellence of the smaller and better-funded University of California system.

He met the challenge by devising a master plan—which was actually called the Master Plan—for higher education in California and then, in 1960, persuading the state legislature to pass it. The plan created a pyramidal three-tier system: the university, the state colleges, and California's community colleges, with each tier much larger than the one above it. The size of each part of the system was based on Kerr's calculations of the capabilities of California's population and of the labor needs of the state's various business sectors. He avoided the most obvious early-in-life sorting aspect of the plan by permitting outstanding students to transfer upward from tier to tier. The Master Plan made Kerr into an overnight national hero because of its headline premise: California would now lead the country and the world into a new kind of democratic society, in which every citizen would receive a public higher education, free of charge. This was an almost unimaginably ambitious premise, which obscured the other main feature of the Master Plan, its protection of the University of California from the academic and budgetary encroachments of the state colleges, via a strict and inviolable rank ordering that was built into the system.

In 1947, shortly before the establishment of ETS, the College Board opened a branch office in Berkeley. That was a sign of the board's national aspirations, and of the University of California's high status in public higher education. Kerr was soon invited to join the ETS board of trustees. Still, it took two decades for the University of California to require the SAT of all its applicants. At the time the College Board office in Berkeley opened, the university was not highly selective. It had not completed the transition to research university status. Like several other state public university systems, it was responsible for accrediting high schools, and this process, rather than standardized testing, was the primary way California managed the fit between high school applicants and university entrants. As the university, and especially its flagship campuses in Berkeley and Los Angeles, became more nationally prominent, it began attracting more out-of-state applicants. For them, there was no institutional connection between high school and the University of California. In 1958, ETS and the College Board began offering the SAT free of charge to all non-California residents who applied to the university. Then, in 1962, the university abruptly dropped the SAT entirely, causing high alarm at ETS and the College Board.

But the university-protecting logic of the Master Plan inexorably pushed the university in the direction of standardized admissions tests. In 1963, the university stopped accrediting high schools. Although the Master Plan promised admission to the university to the top eighth of California public high school graduates, population growth, grade inflation, and the end of the direct link between the university and high schools meant that Berkeley and the University of California, Los Angeles, at least, could no longer accept all eligible applicants. There had to be a way, preferably not highly expensive or logistically challenging, of choosing which ones to admit. In 1968 the university finally began requiring the SAT of all applicants.

The University of California was the SAT's most important client, but the logic of SAT adoption pertained at other state university systems. The test had the allure of association with Harvard and other elite universities. It regularized and made less labor and cost intensive the process of reviewing applications; even though universities were officially not supposed to use cutoff scores and automatically turn down lower-scoring applicants, many did. Perhaps most important, the tests were seen as an aid in transitioning one's institution to the research university model, with the prestige that entailed. A system in which the direct link between state universities and high schools was broken, in which fewer students were admitted and most graduated, in which remediation and mentoring were not required of most faculty members, and in which the definition of a good student was one who had the same high academic skill that faculty members had—all that was highly attractive to faculty members whose primary orientation was toward their research.

The test that colleges now treat as interchangeable with the SAT as an admissions device, the ACT (which used to stand for American College Testing), began in 1958 as a direct challenge to the SAT and everything it stood for. The ACT's father was E. F. Lindquist of the University of Iowa. He believed that tests standing between high school and college should measure academic achievement, not something akin to IQ, which was a concept he rejected, and that they should be used for placement, not selection. All through the 1960s, the ACT and SAT competed to sign up universities. The SAT's territory was more on the coasts and the ACT's more in the middle of the country, the SAT's more private universities and the ACT's more public universities, and the SAT's more selective research universities and the ACT's more open-admissions, teaching-oriented universities. Other, now long forgotten, private companies were also trying to establish themselves in the booming higher education admissions testing business. But the net effect of all this activity, over the long term, was less that different visions emerged of what tests measured and what they should be used for, and more that admissions testing became universalized in higher education. Standardized admissions tests sealed their dominance as the national gatekeepers between high school and a selective college.

What has become a familiar drama followed the passage of the California Master Plan. First came a highly visible internal protest movement from the Left, the Free Speech Movement, which was objecting, in part, to the university's bureaucratization and to its ties to the federal government's Cold War research funding system. Then came a far more consequential political counterreaction from the Right, symbolized by the election of Ronald Reagan as governor of California in 1966. One of Reagan's signature campaign promises, and early official actions, was firing Kerr. More gradually, the California state colleges mustered enough ambition and political strength to transform themselves into the California State University system, breaking through the confines the Master Plan had placed on them. And partly because of California's increasing population and demographic diversity, especially after the federal government adopted a more liberal immigration policy in 1965, the number of students who wanted to attend California's higher education system rose dramatically while the political consensus around generous state support for the system was eroding. In the 1970s the University of California began charging tuition, even to California residents. By the 1980s admission to the most prestigious University of California campuses had become highly competitive and therefore also highly contentious. All this raised profound educational and political questions that remain pressing today: What is the relationship between elite higher education and mass higher education? How can universities maintain the loyal support of the political system, as a proxy for the general public, while excluding more people than they include? As Kerr himself put it back in the early 1960s, "The great university is of necessity elitist—the elite of merit—but it operates in an environment dedicated to an egalitarian philosophy. How may the contribution of the elite be made clear to the egalitarians, and how may an aristocracy in intellect justify itself to all men?"[7]

CHAPTER 3

Testing, Affirmative Action, and the Law

IN THE SAME YEARS after the Second World War when higher education was expanding and standardized admissions testing was becoming commonplace, the civil rights movement was breaking through the academic elite's previous blindness to (or participation in) racism in America. Universities have survived for as long as they have because they can adapt to changes in society. In this case, the overwhelmingly white selective universities decided beginning in the mid-1960s to integrate themselves. Not without internal contention, but without a great deal of external compulsion, they adopted affirmative action policies that wound up increasing the Black presence in their student bodies and faculties—above what it had been, but usually below proportionality to the national population.

For reasons that W. Allison Davis and Robert Havighurst identified back in 1948,[1] this new goal was not in harmony with the adoption of standardized tests in admissions; there is a persistent, though shrinking, Black-white gap in average test scores, reflecting the gap in the lived experiences of the races in the United States. Admission purely, or primarily, by test score would produce less racially integrated student bodies, not the more integrated student bodies the selective universities had begun to want. For complex institutions like research universities, this did not represent an insuperable problem; as we have seen, these universities have always balanced multiple goals that are not perfectly aligned with each other, while moving generally forward. But the combination of standardized testing and affirmative action generated a vulnerability to lawsuits. A white plaintiff could claim that in turning him down while accepting Black applicants with lower test scores, a university had violated the Fourteenth Amendment to the Constitution or the Civil Rights Act of 1964, legal milestones that, in service to the cause of progress for Black Americans, forbade discrimination on the basis of race.

Just a few years after the advent of affirmative action, Marco DeFunis, a rejected white applicant to the University of Washington's law school, sued the university. His was the first of a decades-long series of cases to come before the U.S. Supreme Court, all using test scores to make the argument that affirmative action is a form of antiwhite discrimination. The Court had great difficulty in making a decision; in 1974, it finally declared the case moot because DeFunis, who had been admitted to the University of Washington law school under the order of a lower court, was now close to graduation. The Court, which had issued a clear, unanimous ruling in the *Brown v. Board of Education* case on segregated schools in 1954, has never, through nearly fifty years of cases, been able to find its way to an unmistakable consensus position on affirmative action in admissions—including in its most recent decision striking down affirmative action. The justices are themselves products of the highly selective elite law school pipeline, even more so now than when the string of affirmative action cases began (eight of the nine current justices went to law school at either Harvard or Yale, and all nine served as clerks to federal judges). Even the fiery liberals among them can have a hard time seeing the system that produced them as unfair. In the *DeFunis* case, Justice William O. Douglas, a crusader who was rarely plagued by doubt, produced eleven separate drafts of an opinion, in the aggregate taking just about every position on affirmative action that one could possibly take: for racial quotas, for "colorblindness," for abolishing tests, for admission by lottery.

The signals emerging from the *DeFunis* case were not encouraging for the civil rights community. Mainstream Jewish organizations, formerly reliably liberal, now saw affirmative action as a harbinger of a possible return of the old, hated Jewish quotas at universities, so they took DeFunis's side. Alexander Bickel of Yale Law School, one of the country's most prominent legal scholars, who as a young Supreme Court law clerk had drafted a crucial internal memo in support of the 1954 *Brown* decision, wrote an anti–affirmative action friend of the court brief on behalf of the American Jewish Committee. The sociologist Nathan Glazer wrote a book called *Affirmative Discrimination*. The opinion that Douglas finally published treated affirmative action as unconstitutional; the Fourteenth Amendment, he wrote, "commands the elimination of racial barriers, not their creation in order to satisfy our theory as to how society ought to be organized."[2]

That was the background for the next, and until now the most important, Supreme Court affirmative action case—which, like so many other milestones in the history of American higher education, originated in California. In *Bakke v. Regents of the University of California*, Allan Bakke, a rejected white applicant to the University of California at Davis's medical school, sued because the school had set aside sixteen places in its entering class of one hundred for minority applicants only. The case drew intense public attention. There were more "friend of the court" briefs filed than in any previous Supreme Court case. On the day it was argued—October 12, 1977—people lined up for hours in advance in the hope of getting a seat, as if the *Bakke* case were a Bruce Springsteen concert. Inside the Court, it quickly became clear that Lewis Powell, a Republican lawyer from Richmond, Virginia, was the swing vote, so he was assigned to write the opinion. The clerk Powell asked to draft his opinion in the case was Robert Comfort, who is now retired after a long career as a tax lawyer, first at a big firm and then at Amazon. "In Powell's view, the best result was to preserve affirmative action in some form," Comfort told me. "He told me that. He said, 'I want to find a middle ground. My client, the country, needs for this to be the result. How do we get there?'"[3]

Powell disliked the system that the medical school had created, explicitly reserving places for minority applicants. "There was no chance of Powell supporting Davis," Comfort said. "The way the places got set aside was, the student groups got together and horse-traded. Powell thought that was offensive—to let politics decide how to cut up the melon." Four justices were willing to support the university's version of affirmative action, and one of those who wasn't, John Paul Stevens, was moving to the left and might have provided a fifth vote if the case had arrived a few years later. Powell's biographer, John Jeffries, has written that even Powell, despite what he told Comfort, considered supporting Davis—until, in a conference, Thurgood Marshall, the Court's only Black justice, said that some form of formal racial recompense would be necessary for the next hundred years. "The remark left Powell speechless," Jeffries writes; it gave Powell "a sharpened sense of the vast gulf that separated him from the liberals."[4]

So it fell to Comfort to find an argument for keeping affirmative action, while also banning the use of race in admissions as openly as Davis had. He burrowed into the stack of friend of the court briefs, looking for something that would help. "There were a lot of really bad briefs," he said. "A lot of them were just terrible." But one stood out—produced by Harvard, the same university that had successfully pioneered and promoted the adoption of standardized admissions tests a few decades earlier. "The Harvard brief offered the middle ground Powell was looking for." And that was legally enshrining the principle of diversity, as an intellectually enriching quality that universities' student bodies ought to have. The memo about the case that Comfort wrote for Powell said, "Educational Diversity—This seems to be the step in the analysis offering the best opportunity for taking a middle course." Powell's decision quoted extensively from Harvard's brief. Harvard therefore wound up as the originator of admissions by standardized aptitude testing, and also of the diversity justification for affirmative action—and from within the institution, those two positions didn't seem contradictory, because they had in common a large institutional ambition and an insistence on autonomy.

Diversity became such a consequential concept—for forty-five years, it was the one legally permissible way to address the contradiction between standardized admissions tests and racial integration at selective universities—that it has attracted a great deal of close attention. No one has devoted more time to it than David Oppenheimer, a veteran civil rights lawyer and teacher at Berkeley law school. Like a lot of civil rights lawyers, Oppenheimer spent much of his career feeling frustrated with diversity being the legal foundation on which something as important as integrating elite higher education had to rest. There were other possible justifications for affirmative action, and this one seemed to understand the benefit of more Black students on campus as being mainly that they would enrich the experience of the white students. Oppenheimer, a quiet man who doesn't have the manner one associates with a crusader but who is hard to deter once he gets the bit in his teeth, decided to embark on a quest to find out where the word had come from. Maybe, he thought, if he could find its source, something crucial about race, education, and the law in America would be revealed.

Oppenheimer was struck by how ubiquitous the concept of diversity had become. It was the basis of subsequent Supreme Court decisions on affirmative action for forty years, a guiding principle in the admissions and hiring policies of essentially all universities, and also a goal widely adopted, at least rhetorically, in corporations, in the arts, in the military—nearly everywhere. Oppenheimer assumed that the nonlegal world had gotten the term from the legal world, but what was its origin in the legal world? It had never previously appeared in any court decision or piece of legislation that he could find.[5] He discovered that in the *DeFunis* case, Harvard had submitted two different friend of the court briefs to the Supreme Court, and the one that had focused on diversity somehow hadn't wound up in the official court record or in any of the standard legal databases. The principal author of the brief was Archibald Cox, a Harvard law professor who had recently been fired from the Nixon administration during the Watergate "Saturday night massacre." When Cox returned to Cambridge, Harvard's new president, Derek Bok, asked him to write the brief. A few years later, during the *Bakke* case, Harvard persuaded the University of California to let Cox, rather than its own lawyer, argue on its behalf in the Supreme Court.

Only one person who worked on the brief with Cox is still alive: James Bierman, a Washington lawyer who was a twenty-eight-year-old associate dean of admissions at Harvard Law School when Cox asked him to produce a first draft. In those days, Bierman told me, a typical Harvard Law School class had only four or five Black students out of four hundred. For most of its history, Harvard Law School had not been highly selective. A third of each entering class would flunk out.[6] After the Law School Admission Test (LSAT) was introduced in 1948 and applications soared, admissions became much tighter, and test scores became a direct barrier to an increased Black presence. Bierman said, "We had to do something deliberately, because of racism in this country. Discrimination has been taking place for as long as people have been alive, or even *in utero*. You have an applicant pool where the objective numbers for Blacks and whites do not look the same. How do we justify accepting someone with a lower LSAT score?"[7] He took language from a report that the Harvard undergraduate admissions office had produced in 1960 about how it selected students, which didn't mention race but did mention the goal of creating a student body that would include people of different talents and backgrounds—including a hypothetical "Idaho farm boy." (One of Harvard's former deans of admissions was himself a former Idaho farm boy.) This took Harvard off the hook of having to apply a single academic standard to all applicants, and it was easy to add racial diversity to the list of qualities the university was looking for. In Comfort's memo to Justice Powell about the *Bakke* case, next to the passage where Comfort brought up diversity, there is a handwritten notation by Powell: "This is [a] position that appealed to me in *DeFunis*."[8]

After uncovering all this, Oppenheimer was still unsatisfied. Surely the principle of diversity must have deeper, and specifically racial, roots. As he kept looking, he came across what he considers the Rosetta Stone of diversity, the key to understanding the principle as we have understood it in recent decades. It is a slim pamphlet, published in 1957, called *The Open Universities in South Africa*. At the time, South Africa had two universities that admitted Black students, but the apartheid government was preparing legislation that would force them to segregate. The top officials of the University of Cape Town, which was one of the integrated universities, organized an opposing campaign—the pamphlet was part of that. South Africa's integrated universities, the pamphlet said, "believe that racial diversity within the university is essential to the ideal of a university in a multi-racial society." It went on,

"Nowadays it is almost axiomatic that a university should be more diverse in its membership than is the community in which it exists. The diversity itself contributes to the discovery of truth, for truth is hammered out in discussion, in the class of ideas."[9] The pamphlet not only identified diversity as a justification for racial integration, it also placed the issue in the context of universities' historical claim to academic freedom and protection from political interference.

Oppenheimer discovered that T. B. Davie, who held the title of principal at the University of Cape Town, had gotten a grant from the Carnegie Corporation to travel to the United States and talk to prominent educators about the material that wound up in the pamphlet. Davie visited Harvard Law School and met with the dean there, Erwin Griswold. Oppenheimer located a diary that Davie kept during his trip, in which he wrote that he and Griswold had discussed the importance of racial diversity. Albert Centlivres, the chief justice of South Africa and the chancellor of the University of Cape Town, also got a travel grant from Carnegie. Through that he met Supreme Court Justice Felix Frankfurter, who then quoted at length from the *Open Universities* pamphlet in an opinion he wrote in a free speech case in 1957. Frankfurter was a former Harvard Law School professor, still very much in touch with his former colleagues. Oppenheimer also found a letter mentioning racial diversity that another Harvard law professor, Paul Freund, had written in 1959. So he assumes, without having found an indisputable smoking-gun connection, that long before the *DeFunis* and *Bakke* cases, Cox, as a Harvard law school faculty member, had been exposed to the idea of racial diversity as something universities should care about.

Oppenheimer's search left him far more kindly disposed to diversity than he had been at the beginning. He now sees it as a way of placing affirmative action at the center of a long project, dating back centuries, of protecting universities' sacred place in the world, so that they have, in the words of South Africa's *Open Universities* pamphlet, "the rights to decide what may be taught, how it may be taught, who may teach, and who may study."[10] Diversity's constant use as a central principle by many other institutions today, not just by universities, underscores how influential universities can be outside their own campuses—they're the ones who introduced it. In the immediate aftermath of the Supreme Court's *Bakke* decision, Oppenheimer says, there wasn't much attention paid to this crucial word—its inherent power has been demonstrated only over time. And with the Court's 2023 decision in cases involving, again, Harvard, and also the University of North Carolina, its future is in question, inside and outside universities.

Oppenheimer, and a wide range of universities and other institutions, may have been convinced of the importance of diversity, but the entire country never was. One can tick off a series of objections to it as the core principle around which remedies for something as deeply rooted and pervasive as racism in America have to be organized. Back in 1978, most of institutional Black America would have preferred that the Supreme Court had simply endorsed the University of California's policy of reserving places for minority applicants. The *Amsterdam News*'s headline after the decision was "We Lost." Powell's decision insisted that any use of race in admissions be subject to strict scrutiny, meaning, legally, that unlike all of the other standard admissions preferences, it would be presumed to be unconstitutional unless universities could offer an extraordinary justification. Many white liberals' rhetoric at the time about affirmative action assumed that because the Jim Crow system had recently been eliminated, racism would soon disappear as a problem in American life, so affirmative action could be a temporary fix, a bridge to take the country from its racist past to its nonracist present. A Supreme Court sanction for explicitly racial admissions would have been an acknowledgment of racism as an ongoing present-day reality. It would also have made the conflict between test scores and the creation of a more integrated student body much less sharp. Diversity as the only permissible justification for affirmative action amounted to an invitation to future lawsuits and other attacks, because it didn't make it clear that programs explicitly favoring Black people, unlike programs explicitly favoring other categories of people, are okay.

Universities that use standardized tests and also have affirmative action policies hate being statistically specific about the extent of their commitment to affirmative action, but that's partly because of the direction in which the Supreme Court has pushed them. (One study published in 2009 estimated that at selective private colleges, the effect of being Black on one's chance of admission is the equivalent of adding 310 points to one's combined SAT scores; at the University of California in 2019, Black admitted students had average SAT scores 156 points lower, and admitted Latino students 214 points lower, than those of admitted Asian students.[11]) The plain truth is that affirmative action was a direct result of the civil rights movement and was aimed at racially integrating universities. The diversity justification for it dances around that obvious fact and so generates a good deal of cognitive dissonance. As Jamal Greene, a professor at Columbia Law School, writes in his recent book *How Rights Went Wrong*, "The Supreme Court's distaste for overt race-conscious admissions plans doesn't, of course, mean that those plans don't exist. It just means that instead of acknowledging structural racial inequality and tailoring their programs to the metes and bounds of that special social problem, schools—with the Court's blessing—pursue racial justice in the shadows. . . . All American schools that take race into consideration claim to do so because it's crucial to their 'diversity' efforts. This isn't quite hogwash, but it's close."[12]

Standardized tests were not intentionally designed to exclude Black applicants, and they don't generally underpredict Black applicants' grades as they begin college, but the more they become dispositive in admissions, the lower the Black presence becomes. Berkeley's dropped by 50 percent the first year that an anti–affirmative action initiative was implemented in California. Harvard's, according to one person who has worked with the plaintiffs in the case that the Supreme Court decided in 2023, would drop by two-thirds. Affirmative action has always been, in fact, racially motivated. And affirmative action has produced the intended result: far more substantially racially integrated elite universities, and far more substantial racial integration of the world into which elite university admission leads.

It has become standard for members of the Black elite, from Barack and Michelle Obama on down, to reflect ruefully on the role of affirmative action in their Ivy League education—it helped with access on the one hand and generated annoying perceptions about them on the other—but it has helped create a Black leadership class, outside the confines of a separate Black America, that hadn't existed before. David Garrow's massive biography of Barack Obama says that when he applied to transfer from Occidental College to Columbia University, and again when he applied for membership in the *Harvard Law Review*, he declined to check the box indicating his race—and also that the reason he wanted to join the law review in the first place was to demonstrate that he hadn't been an affirmative action admit to Harvard Law School. An environment of extremely ambitious and competitive people who perceive the handing out of rewards as a zero-sum game and who are exquisitely attuned to the question of who truly deserves them doesn't make for a natural, comfortable fit with a not perfectly congruent social-reform priority. In a 1982 book, the Harvard philosopher Michael Sandel imagined this letter being written to a rejected applicant: "It is not your fault that when you came along society happened not to need the qualities you had to offer. Those admitted instead of you were not themselves deserving of a place, nor worthy of praise for the factors that led to their admission. We are in any case only using them—and you—as instruments of a wider social purpose."[13]

Robert Comfort, Powell's law clerk, reflecting on Powell's decision in the *Bakke* case, said, "It was not the most elegant piece of legal reasoning, but it was the right result. The mainstream press reaction to the decision was overwhelmingly positive. We had saved the country from another civil war. The academic reactions, on both sides, were very harshly critical. Sometimes the right answer is not the intellectually defensible answer. It's not the lawyerly answer. It's a compromise. A lawyer isn't interested in producing the clearest opinion. He wants to produce the best result."[14] Comfort's assertion is supported by the fact that most of the public opponents of affirmative action have endorsed the goal of racial integration, while insisting that it should be achieved by means that do not explicitly take race into account. When the Supreme Court heard the arguments in the most recent affirmative action cases, even the lawyers for the plaintiffs and the conservative justices were unwilling to advocate for a "colorblind" admissions policy that would produce a radically resegregated result; instead, one saw on display the impulse to find a nonracial criterion that produces at least some enhanced degree of racial integration, while treating explicit racial preferences as uniquely unacceptable.

In addition to the legal challenges to affirmative action, there have been political challenges. In the early 1990s, two conservative California academics, Glynn Custred and Tom Wood, launched a ballot initiative to ban affirmative action in all activities conducted by the state, including higher education admissions. Coming at a moment of conservative resurgence and liberal retreat nationally, the initiative got a great deal of attention. President Bill Clinton made it known that he felt torn about affirmative action and appointed a group at the White House to study it. At the end of this process, Clinton made a speech whose most memorable line was, "Mend it, don't end it." The phrasing indicated that he found the practice of affirmative action flawed, so it hardly counted as a ringing defense. The initiative, called Proposition 209, was on the ballot in California in 1996, the year Clinton was running for reelection. He did not campaign against it. Both Proposition 209 and Clinton won easily on Election Day. Since 1996, initiatives to ban affirmative action have been on the ballot in seven states; each one has passed. In 2020, the voters of majority-minority California, while they were supporting Joe Biden over Donald Trump by a nearly thirty-point margin, decisively voted down a ballot initiative that would have overturned Proposition 209 and reinstituted affirmative action.

In the Supreme Court, the 1978 *Bakke* decision withstood two direct challenges. The next case after *Bakke*, in 2003, involved the University of Michigan. In another split decision, the Court rejected an undergraduate affirmative action policy that favored minority applicants in an explicitly numerical way by a five-to-four vote but accepted a law school policy that was "holistic" in its use of race as a plus factor in admissions, also by a five-to-four vote. Justice Sandra Day O'Connor's decision in the Michigan cases, noting that many corporate and military leaders[15] had petitioned the Supreme Court not to strike down affirmative action, declared that "the path to leadership must be visibly open to talented and qualified individuals of every race and ethnicity."[16] This was a justification that went far beyond just promoting diversity on campus and is more accurately descriptive of what affirmative action is intended to do and does. But O'Connor also wrote, "The Court expects that 25 years from now, the use of racial preferences will no longer be necessary." Eleven years after she wrote that, Michael Brown was killed in Ferguson, Missouri, and a new era of enhanced activism against racism began. Fourteen years afterward, O'Connor told her biographer, Evan Thomas, that the twenty-five-year deadline "may have been a misjudgment."[17]

In Texas, another lawsuit challenging affirmative action filed in the early 1990s was decided by the federal Fifth Circuit Court of Appeals in favor of the plaintiff, Cheryl Hopwood. The Supreme Court declined to hear the case, which meant it had the same effect in Texas as Proposition 209 in California—an affirmative action ban. The University of Texas decided it could avoid the major reductions in minority students that had followed Proposition 209 by establishing a policy under which any student who had graduated in the top 10 percent of a high school class would be automatically admitted, with no reference to test scores. This policy, ratified by the Texas legislature, took race into account implicitly but not explicitly: because Texas high schools were highly segregated, it would allow for the top students at minority high schools to be admitted, in a way that got around the conflict between admissions tests and integration. Then, in 2003, the University of Texas took the Supreme Court's Michigan decision as a strong enough affirmation of the diversity standard that it began, in addition to its 10 percent policy, to take race into account explicitly. It could, for example, accept a Black applicant from a high-rated, majority-white high school who fell below the top 10 percent of the class.

That led to another lawsuit filed by a rejected white applicant, Abigail Fisher, which came before the Supreme Court twice, first in 2013 and then in 2016. Again the Court affirmed the diversity standard in a split decision, which was again written by a relatively moderate Republican justice—in this instance, Anthony Kennedy. The decision drew a long, stinging dissent from a more conservative Republican justice, Samuel Alito, who took the unusual step of reading out loud from the bench a section of his opinion. "This is affirmative action gone wild," he wrote about the University of Texas's admissions system. He ended his dissent this way:

> What is at stake is whether university administrators may justify systematic racial discrimination simply by asserting that such discrimination is necessary to achieve the educational benefits of diversity, without explaining—much less proving—why the discrimination is needed or how the discriminatory plan is well crafted to serve its objectives. Even though UT has never provided any coherent explanation for its asserted need to discriminate on the basis of race, and even though UT's position relies on a series of unsupported and noxious racial assumptions, the majority concludes that UT has met its heavy burden. This conclusion is remarkable—and remarkably wrong.[18]

At this point affirmative action in admissions had the enthusiastic backing of the universities that practiced it, but it did not have public support and it was hanging by a thread legally. The Supreme Court, over the decades, had steadily narrowed the justification for it: the only permissible grounds was diversity, it had to meet a strict scrutiny test, the clock was ticking on Justice O'Connor's dictum about a deadline, and it had never been able to get strong majority support on the Court. A vocal minority of the justices were bitterly opposed. And the Court was changing. The authors of the decisions upholding affirmative action, Justices O'Connor and Kennedy, retired. For twelve years—2010 to 2022—no justice appointed by a Democratic president joined the Court, and in that time three justices appointed by President Donald Trump joined, all ideologically conservative, none who have spent long years as practical-minded practicing lawyers like Lewis Powell. The chief justice, John Roberts, has been a consistent opponent of affirmative action. So in January 2022, when the Court agreed to hear two more cases challenging affirmative action in admissions, the one against Harvard and another against the University of North Carolina, it was clear what the result would be.

The Harvard case had a somewhat different central argument from the previous Supreme Court cases seeking to overturn affirmative action. The plaintiff is not a rejected white applicant but Asian American applicants as a class. Asians are the ethnic group rising fastest in their representation in selective universities—they are at about 25 percent of the student body at Harvard, and about 40 percent at Berkeley—but if admission were solely by test scores, they might be a majority of the student body, as they are at some selective public high schools that use admissions tests. Also, the evidence in this case that got the most public attention was not SAT or ACT scores but a "personal score" that the Harvard admissions office gave applicants, on which Asians on average ranked lower than other applicants. (One can safely bet that Harvard will stop assigning personal scores to applicants in the future.) This gave the case some distance from the by now long-running debates about standardized testing and race.

Still, when the decision and the concurrences and dissents came down, they were about race. That was inevitable, legally, because the Harvard and North Carolina lawsuits were based on the argument that affirmative action violated the Fourteenth Amendment and the 1964 Civil Rights Act—measures that were created to confer full citizenship on Black Americans and whose wording bans discrimination on the basis of race. The conservative justices who wrote opinions saw these measures as belonging to a long-running national commitment to "colorblindness" that can now finally become a controlling principle. The liberal justices saw them as color conscious, in the context of their times, and as belonging to a long and honorable tradition of reparative policies that amounted, and still amount, to insufficient pushback against a much larger and long-running number of policies that have been color conscious in the other direction. There's not much room for agreement about these fundamental matters, but right now the conservatives have enough votes to win. The decisions in the Harvard and North Carolina cases evidently bring to an end the long reign of the diversity standard in higher education admissions, at least as it pertains to race, and so make it much harder for universities to continue pursuing their preferred course of embracing both standardized tests and racial integration. They will have to choose one or the other. Some selective institutions have chosen to reinstitute test requirements, usually without publicly addressing what the consequences of their decision on the Black presence in their student bodies will be; others will probably opt to join what has become a substantial sector of the higher education system without required standardized college admissions tests for the first time in three-quarters of a century. What will that mean?

CHAPTER 4

Admissions without Testing

JUST AS THE UNIVERSITY OF CALIFORNIA was the SAT's most hoped-for new client at the outset, the target of the most important legal challenge to affirmative action three decades later, and the target of the most important electoral challenge two decades after that, it has also been the pioneer in moving away from standardized admissions tests.

In 2001, Richard Atkinson, a cognitive psychologist who was president of the University of California, gave a speech in which he harshly criticized the SAT and announced that he was considering dropping it as a requirement for applicants to the university.[1] This got the world's attention, because Atkinson was the SAT's number-one customer. Back in the late 1940s, W. Allison Davis and Robert Havighurst were lonely voices of skepticism about standardized testing; by the early 1970s, criticism of standardized tests in general and the SAT in particular had become a frequent cause among education reformers on the left. But this was different, because nobody at Atkinson's level of official prominence had joined the chorus.

As Atkinson told the story, his road-to-Damascus moment came during a visit to his grandchildren, when he found his granddaughter, then in sixth grade, assiduously preparing for the SAT by studying lists of analogies. Organized test prep had begun many decades earlier, personified by Stanley Kaplan, a Brooklyn schoolteacher who offered classes in his basement on how to raise your scores. One of Atkinson's quarrels with the SAT was that the main source of research on the test was its own purveyors, ETS and the College Board, which were hardly disinterested parties. They had insisted for decades that it would be impossible to prepare for the SAT, but meanwhile test prep continued to grow, so obviously test takers and their families did not accept the test makers' position. And test prep was a private industry, therefore much more accessible to people with means than to people without. It had spread by the turn of the millennium to the point that Atkinson's granddaughter was already prepping, many years before she would actually take the SAT.

Another point that troubled Atkinson was the connection between the SAT and IQ testing. Publicly, ETS and the College Board insisted that the SAT was a test of "developed ability," not intelligence, and eventually they removed the word "aptitude" from its title so that SAT became an acronym with no words behind it. But as a high official in American higher education, Atkinson had been in private meetings where testing officials had presented the SAT as essentially an intelligence test. IQ tests have a highly charged history, because of their historical association with eugenics, their use in educational tracking systems, and the racial gaps they display. SATs were widely believed by high school students to be a measurement of "how smart you are"—that's why nobody, it seems, ever forgets their SAT score. Their presumed importance sent a signal that prepping is more consequential than learning the material being taught in your courses at school. Atkinson strongly favored achievement tests—tests measuring mastery of a curriculum—over aptitude tests. His immediate proposal was that the University of California switch from requiring the SAT to requiring what were then known as SAT IIs, subject-matter tests also produced by ETS and the College Board.

The College Board was then headed by a politician, Gaston Caperton, a former governor of West Virginia, whose instinct was not to dig in his heels but to compromise. He ordered a wholesale revision of the SAT, to bring it closer into the range of being an achievement test. (For example, the analogies that Atkinson had found his granddaughter studying were dropped, and an essay was added.) In return, the University of California kept the SAT as an admissions requirement.

But the tide was running in the other direction. California at the time of the passage of Clark Kerr's Master Plan was 92 percent white; today it's 35 percent white. The majority of California public school graduates are Latino or Black. This, combined with the long-running effects of Proposition 209, generates unending pressure on a University of California system that is two-thirds white and Asian American, and the pressure has fallen specifically on the use of standardized admissions tests. After the passage of Proposition 209, the university instituted a series of changes meant to combat its negative effects on the minority presence at its most prestigious campuses. These included emphasizing high school grades more, adding other admissions criteria, and beefing up admissions staffs to the point where each applicant's folder could be read qualitatively. Atkinson's preferred reform, an achievement-oriented standardized testing regime, fell by the wayside; within a few years, the College Board and ETS had eliminated some of the revisions to the SAT that they had made in response to Atkinson's critique, like the required essay, and in 2021 they stopped offering the SAT II, the test series that Atkinson preferred to the main SAT, entirely.[2]

In 2019, partly in response to a lawsuit filed by a civil rights group, Janet Napolitano, the president of the University of California, ordered a review of the use of standardized tests in admissions. The university initially suspended the use of tests, and then, in 2021, it announced that it would no longer consider standardized test scores in admissions at all, permanently. The California State University system quickly followed suit. These decisions came at a time when the number of colleges and universities nationwide that had adopted test-optional policies or suspended their test requirements had grown from a trickle to a torrent, especially because of the coincidence of the COVID-19 pandemic and the racial reckoning that followed the murder of George Floyd. It's likely that many colleges and universities had been waiting to see how the Supreme Court would rule on the current legal challenges to affirmative action. The University of California may once again, in dropping tests entirely, wind up being the leader of a national trend.

In the technical sense, the SAT is designed to predict academic performance in college, and it is evaluated on the basis of how well it does that. The test of the test is a process called validation: comparisons of students' test scores with their academic records in college, to determine how closely the two match. Over the decades, there have been many validity studies of the SAT, by ETS and the College Board and by independent researchers, that measure its relation to first-semester college grades, first-year grades, and, sometimes, graduation rates, across a broad range of institutions. To make a very long story short, the SAT's predictive validity is highest for the short term; it falls off over the full length of college. A typical short-term predictive validity coefficient (R) would be just above 0.40, which would mean that the SAT predicts just above 15 percent (R-squared) of the variation in short-term grades. Anthony Carnevale, who spent ten years as a vice president of ETS, with responsibility for managing its public controversies, and who now directs a research center at Georgetown University, told me, "All we had was, we can predict first-year grades. That was it. And we couldn't call it aptitude."[3]

To a testing enthusiast, it is a small miracle that a test can, after just a few hours with a student, make a meaningful, if not all-powerful, prediction about how well that student will do academically in the short-term future. But it should be obvious that the SAT's predictive power has a lot to do with the student's circumstances, educational and otherwise, in high school and before. There are not a lot of people from poor families and poor schools who nonetheless get superb scores on the SAT. The SAT is not designed to answer the question of who most deserves one of the limited number of slots in selective colleges, or who should be designated early in life as a future leader. It is designed to predict first-year grades. I will discuss the social and political implications of admissions testing in the next chapter. For now, I will focus on the tests themselves; they, not the purpose and vision behind them, are what people notice about admissions testing. There are a series of questions about them that have come up consistently over the years and so have given rise to serious research. It's worth going through some of these.

First, is the SAT biased? Bear in mind, again, that the SAT is validated against academic performance in college. Therefore, in the technical sense, just demonstrating that there are gaps by race, ethnicity, class, or gender on test scores doesn't prove that a test is biased. To do that, one would have to show that test scores for the group on the lower side of the scoring gap underpredict that group's performance in college. Test makers call each question on a test an "item." Not only the test as a whole but each individual item is evaluated for its predictive validity and for whether it produces unusually large gaps by race, class, and gender. The reason tests have unscored sections is so that new items can be introduced and tested before they are used in scored tests.

"Differential item functioning" is the form of bias that test makers aim to avoid. It refers to test questions that produce score gaps that are not predictive of college academic performance. An item with a high differential item functioning shouldn't be used on a test, but an item that produces racial, gender, or class gaps that are the same as the gaps between those groups on the test as a whole, and in academic performance, is assumed to be legitimate. Another way of putting this is to say that students who come from high schools that are academically and socially similar to elite colleges are likely to do better academically when they enter an elite college than are students who come from high schools that are quite different from elite colleges. The predictiveness of the SAT and other tests is higher for first-year grades than for graduation rates, because graduation rates are less a function of a student's immediate level of preparation for college.

In 2003, a retired ETS researcher named Roy Freedle published a much-discussed article in the *Harvard Educational Review* arguing that the SAT is, in fact, racially biased in the technical sense—especially the verbal section of the test. Freedle experimented with notionally dividing the SAT into halves, a hard half (made up of the items on which test takers were least likely to choose the right answer) and an easy half (made up of items on which getting the right answer was more common). In his experiment, Black test takers overperformed on the hard part of the test and underperformed on the easy part. Freedle's idea about why this happened was that easier items test a student's general cultural familiarity, but harder items test intellectual ability. Black students underperformed on easier items because they often don't live in the same culture as white students; a test purified through elimination of the easy questions would remove the principal cause of the Black-white score gap. Freedle called for a new score, R-SAT (for Revised SAT); he raised the idea that using this might make it possible to eliminate affirmative action while retaining the SAT, without reducing the admission of minority students.

ETS has vigorously challenged Freedle's findings, and there hasn't been any movement to exchange the SAT for the R-SAT. The major response to the conflict between the use of standardized tests in admissions and the drive to integrate higher education has been to make tests optional or to drop them, not to change them. One reason colleges and universities have not pushed harder to change the tests in the hope of eliminating racial gaps is that, on average, admissions tests overpredict Black students' first-year grades. Freedle raised the possibility that introducing the R-SAT would also solve the problem of the Black-white grade gap by altering the selection of Black students; but the more common view is that the grade gap is caused by an unwelcoming atmosphere on campus and by underpreparedness.

Second, would other standardized admissions tests be preferable to the SAT and ACT? When Atkinson began questioning the SAT, and arguing for replacing aptitude tests with achievement tests, he pointed out that the SAT II subject-matter tests predicted applicants' performance at the University of California slightly better than the SAT I, the classic aptitude test. It's important to understand that Atkinson was not primarily motivated by a wish to find the most perfectly predictive admissions test. Instead, he was focused on improving the entire ecosystem that has grown up around testing. Most students who take the SAT will not wind up going to a highly selective college. A test that was initially designed and implemented for elite selection wound up affecting the high school experience of many more people who aren't selected for elite colleges than people who are selected.

What Atkinson dreamed of was not so much a more efficient University of California admissions system as a public high school system in which students, teachers, and parents believed that test scores are closely related to mastering course material. Instead of doing test prep that stands outside the high school learning process, students would simply study harder in school. Instead of perceiving test scores as measuring their intellectual worth, students would perceive them as measuring hard work in courses. Instead of feeling they had to add test prep to the curriculum so that students from modest backgrounds would not be at a disadvantage compared with students whose parents could hire expensive private SAT tutors, high schools would upgrade their regular courses. Atkinson's logic would also apply to Advanced Placement (AP) exams, which the University of California still considers even though it has stopped considering SAT and ACT scores. The AP tests were originally designed, in a similar elite-focused spirit to the SAT, to hasten the progress of extraordinarily accomplished students through college so they could get to graduate school more quickly (hence the name), but they have become a system for high schools to upgrade their courses so that they meet the AP tests' standard. AP test scores have roughly similar predictive power to SAT and ACT scores.

Achievement tests encounter a couple of persistent problems. One is the lack of a national curriculum in the United States. A long-running, elaborate, expensive campaign to create a national curriculum, the Common Core (which in many places would have had a new admissions test called Smarter Balanced associated with it), has been only modestly successful. It has run into heavy ideological opposition on the right and the left, as well as from people and institutions that are accustomed to local control. It is very difficult to institute achievement tests as the main college admissions tests nationally in the absence of a national curriculum. Also, achievement tests activate fierce, long-running debates over such questions as how much autonomy teachers should have and whether schools should be primarily oriented toward teaching students sets of facts or ways of thinking. In our quantitatively obsessed country, as soon as there are numbers available, they become a preoccupation, so achievement test scores wind up being used to rate the performance not only of students but also of schools and individual teachers and, in effect, to control the educational direction of the system. AP tests may be curriculum based, but as soon as they are instituted, schools and teachers who have had little to do with formulating them are pressured to "teach to the test." So they hardly count as a testing system that everybody can love. One reason the small number of high schools that were members of the College Board back in the 1930s strongly supported instituting the SAT as the main college admissions test is that it gave them more freedom to teach whatever they wanted. (Some of these super-elite high schools don't offer AP courses today, unlike most merely elite high schools, which do offer them.) And the familiar class and racial gaps show up on achievement tests as well as aptitude tests.

Third, how well do high school grades alone work as an admissions device? Remember that one initial rationale for using the SAT as an admissions test was the presumed unreliability of high school transcripts in judging a student's readiness for college. The reasons for this should be obvious: there are too many high schools, with too many different levels of resources and educational performance, and they are too prone to grade inflation. So it may seem counterintuitive, at least to fans of standardized testing, that the high school GPA is actually a better predictor of academic performance than test scores, even though the high school population is far larger and more diverse today than it was when standardized college admissions tests were first instituted. It's also the case that, after nearly a century of operating admissions offices that evaluate a national pool of students, selective colleges have gotten to know a wide range of high schools and have a higher level of confidence in the meaning of a high school's grading policies than they did back in the early days. A 2009 study by Kevin Rask and Jill Tiefenthaler, of an unnamed highly selective college, found that the SAT, on average, adds only 3 percent to the predictiveness of the high school transcript.

A lot more data go into a high school GPA than a test score—four years' worth of effort versus a few hours' worth. The GPA picks up persistent, sustained effort across a range of circumstances. And it has the additional advantage of not producing the same wide gaps by class and race that the tests do. Another way of putting this is to say that because where a student goes to high school is so highly affected by class and race, the GPA tends to factor out a lot of class and race automatically by measuring a student's performance in an environment with people of similar background.

Probably the most prolific of all SAT researchers, at least outside of ETS and College Board staff, is Saul Geiser, a sociologist who has worked for many years with the University of California system and who led most of the studies associated with Atkinson's critique of the SAT. Geiser has found consistently that in California, the high school GPA is more predictive of student performance in college than the SAT, especially after the first year. Test scores add significantly, but modestly, to the predictiveness of high school grades. But test scores are much more highly correlated with background factors like family income, race and ethnicity, and parental education than are high school grades. In California, background factors explain more than a third of the variance in SAT scores, and their association with SAT scores has been rising—but they explain less than a tenth of the variance in high school grades. A 2015 study by Geiser showed that among applicants to the University of California, SAT scores had become more strongly associated with race and ethnicity than with either parental education or family income—and that overall, the association of SAT scores with background factors was rising over time. When tests add only modestly to the predictiveness of the high school transcript, and are more closely linked to the background factors that admissions testing was originally meant to factor out, why use them?

In their 2009 book *Crossing the Finish Line*, William G. Bowen, Matthew M. Chingos, and Michael S. McPherson were primarily concerned with the question of college completion at public universities, not student selection at highly selective, mainly private universities that have nearly 100 percent graduation rates. They used a large data set to validate test scores and high school grades against college graduation rates, rather than against short-term college grades. They found that high school grades are consistently far more predictive of graduation than test scores, and that test scores "routinely fail to pass standard tests of statistical significance when included with high school GPA in regressions predicting graduation rates. . . . In the larger set of less selective public universities, there is rarely any significant relationship between SAT/ACT scores and graduation rates . . . and in the half-dozen institutions where there is a mildly significant relationship, it is as likely to be negative as positive."[4] Among other things, this conclusion demonstrates how different tests look depending on what question you're trying to use them to answer. The question of how to improve public university graduation rates was not on the minds of the creators of the admissions testing system.

Fourth, what effect do test-optional policies have on who goes to college and how well they perform there? In 2018, Steven T. Syverson, Valerie W. Franks, and William C. Hiss published a detailed study of test-optional admissions, based on nearly a million student records they obtained from twenty-eight colleges, mostly smaller private nonprofit institutions. They found that adopting a test-optional policy usually increases a college's applications, especially from minority and low-income students, and also increases the proportion of minority and low-income students in the student body. By virtue of increasing applications, going test-optional also makes a college more selective, not less. High school grades predict college grades, and graduation rates for applicants who chose not to submit test scores, quite well—in fact, non-score-submitting minority applicants had a higher graduation rate than score-submitting minority applicants. Among applicants, the decision to submit scores had a far higher correlation with family income and education than it did with eventual grades in college. Accepted applicants who hadn't submitted scores were more likely to need financial aid than accepted students who had submitted scores.

This study was published immediately before a large increase in the number of colleges with test-optional policies. We don't have full results from that yet, but what we know about such policies is consistent with other data about admissions testing in the twenty-first century. Test scores add to the predictiveness of the high school transcript, but not by much; the transcript is the best predictor of college performance. Testing, rather than negating the effects of background as was originally intended, appears now to enhance those effects, far more so than high school grades. It also appears that overreliance on tests in admissions not only depresses the admission of minorities and low-income students, it discourages such students from applying in the first place. (At the University of California, after the elimination of the SAT and ACT, minority applications increased significantly, and so did the minority student presence in the university—evidently without depressing overall student academic performance.) The word seems to be out among high school students that tests function as the opposite of a system of opening up previously closed opportunities. And on campus, test-optional admissions policies don't seem to make it more difficult to assemble an academically capable student body.

CHAPTER 5

Testing without Meritocracy

THE PERSON RESPONSIBLE for introducing the word "meritocracy" into our vocabulary is the British sociologist Michael Young. Young was a policy aide in the Labour Party during and after the Second World War, at a time when the United Kingdom, much later than the United States, was extending its universal public education system upward from the elementary grades into high school. This coincided with the period of liberal enthusiasm for IQ testing. After the war, while the United States was creating an IQ test–based college admissions system, the United Kingdom created an even more consequential IQ-based educational sorting system: the eleven-plus exam, which all students in state-run schools would take on the cusp of adolescence, after which they were sent on either to vocational high schools called secondary moderns or to college preparatory high schools called grammar schools.

By the mid-1950s, Young, who had left the Labour Party and begun a long, distinguished career in social science field research in the East End of London, had become deeply disillusioned with this system, though not for exactly the same reasons we might be today. He was, at that point, still an unrepentant believer in the power of IQ tests to discover intellectual talent, but he was also a socialist who was skeptical of the idea of equal opportunity as a plausible basis of a good society. What was good about the old-fashioned British class system, by his lights, was that it was obviously unfair. This made it possible to build political support for redistributionist policies. His fear about the new British educational system was that it would be *too* fair—that it would over time create a brainy and deserving new elite, and that the success of that project would fatally undercut the case for socialism.

Out of these concerns, Young produced in 1958 an extremely odd book—so odd that he had a difficult time getting it published—called *The Rise of the Meritocracy*, a dystopian fantasy that takes the form of a parody of a dissertation by an imaginary scholar (also named Michael Young). It tells the story of a new, educated upper class, selected via IQ tests and substantially made up of people from humble origins, coming to power in ways that cripple the Labour Party and turn what had been effective working-class political activism into pure anger and resentment. The book ends with a footnote reporting that Michael Young has been killed in a massacre carried out by members of the working class in 2034. That date is not too far away from where we are now, and the idea of a mass of alienated people who are motivated politically in substantial part by their dislike of educated elites is obviously not far-fetched, in the United States and many other countries.

Young coined the term "meritocracy" to warn against it, but, at least in the United States, over time it has come into widespread use, mainly as something positive. The term is meant to stand in contrast to "aristocracy," meaning a domain where the circumstances of birth, not merit, determine success. The etymology of these terms is telling, because "aristocracy" and "meritocracy" mean literally the same thing: rule by the best. Back in 1958, Young felt he couldn't use the word "aristocracy" because of the strong association with inheritance it had taken on over time, so he simply substituted a Latin prefix for the original Greek one to get across what he meant. Perhaps the lesson should be that eventually, any system of distributing rewards runs afoul of the unstoppable urge of prosperous parents to pass their advantages on to their children.

In thinking about testing and higher education, it's important that we not let the positive valence that the word "meritocracy" has taken on—the idea that if a system can be called a meritocracy, then it must be good, period—shut down the discussion. It may be helpful to think about some possible alternative definitions of "meritocracy," because doing so clarifies how particular the definition is that Young, and also many Americans who position themselves as defenders of meritocracy, have used. Joseph Kett's 2013 book *Merit* reminds us that although the word "meritocracy" didn't come into common usage until fairly recently, the word "merit" appears regularly in the writings of the most prominent politicians of the founding period of the United States and consistently thereafter— meaning a variety of different things. The same point can be made globally. Just to give one of many possible examples, within the vastness of Leo Tolstoy's *War and Peace* there are a couple of references to the advent of a competitive examination system for promotion to high-level government and military roles in early nineteenth-century Russia. One exchange between two minor members of the nobility goes like this:

> "I ask you, Count—who will be heads of the departments when everybody has to pass examinations?"
>
> "Those who pass the examinations, I suppose," replied Kochubéy, crossing his legs and glancing round.
>
> "Well, I have Pryánichnikov serving under me, a splendid man, a priceless man, but he's sixty. Is he to go up for examination?"[1]

Kett proposes a useful distinction between "essential merit," a positive quality of an individual person, and "institutional merit," a set of standards established and maintained by an organization or a profession. (You may have had conversations with people who tell you proudly that the place where they work is a meritocracy, by which they mean that they consider it to be open to all, regardless of background, and to reward people based only on good performance.) The definition of both kinds of merit has varied greatly over time and in different circumstances. Nonetheless, in the United States during the second half of the twentieth century, "meritocracy" came to be very often used to denote a standardized test–based system for adjudicating the allocation of what were becoming ever more scarce and precious slots in the most highly selective universities. This understanding of meritocracy collapses the broad concept of merit into something much narrower: stellar academic performance during adolescence. It favors a formal, structured system over a looser, less organized one. It confuses a numerically very small elite selection system with a universal national opportunity structure. It blends Kett's distinct individual and institutional varieties of merit into a single, conceptually blurry concept, and therefore assumes that the purpose of a meritocracy is to make sure that a limited number of rewards, golden tickets to success, are distributed fairly; as Kett quotes a British sociologist, Keith Hope, saying, "When Americans talk about merit, they really mean desert."[2]

As a thought experiment, if we are to understand meritocracy as meaning, simply, that success goes to the deserving, then how about just leaving it to the marketplace? Those who made the most money would be assumed to be those with the most merit. Anyone who is reading this book will likely regard that idea as absurd on its face. What about all of the large and small imperfections that exist in market systems and make them unfair—the favoritism, the self-dealing, the corruption? What about the tendency for the rich to get richer and to pass their advantages on intergenerationally through inheritance and other means? What about the market's overvaluing of some fields and undervaluing of others?

But it's worth asking whether a test-based meritocracy is much less unfair. Does it really, as James Bryant Conant promised back in the 1940s, completely upend the class system once a generation? Does it give every person a completely equal chance to succeed? Does it disable the long-running historical tendency of meritocracies to degrade into aristocracies? Of course not. If you work in an academic setting, it's tempting to see academically determined measures of merit as being less flawed than market-determined measures, but that may just show that the world you've succeeded in, whatever it is, often feels essentially benign. A 2013 quantitative study of a large sample of high school valedictorians by Alexandra Walton Radford showed a very strong association between a family background in the top income quintile and the likelihood of attending one of the country's most selective colleges, even among this cohort of outstanding students. Inside an elite university, one sees highly able students from across a range of backgrounds; this makes the system overall appear to be much less biased toward the prosperous than it actually is.

What if, instead, we defined meritocracy in terms that do entail education but do not entail selection—that is, in terms more consistent with the Truman Commission report? By that definition, we would recognize that higher education is strongly associated with opportunity, and we would conclude that it should be provided to as many people as possible, at as high a level as possible, rather than emphasizing the selection of a lucky few. Promoters of meritocracy often like to use the metaphor of a race, with everybody placed at the same starting line. Empirically, that is wildly undescriptive of American society as it is today, but even in theory, wouldn't it be better if the starting line were the completion of higher education, not the beginning of higher education? Wouldn't it be better if we lived in a society where it mattered that you had finished your education, and where that was a realistic possibility for everybody, but where it didn't matter so much where you had gotten your education, because your performance in whatever work you did would be the determinant of success? It ought to be axiomatic that when a society makes highly consequential, life-shaping choices about people when they are young and still living at home with their parents, it is well-nigh impossible for those choices to be background neutral.

Besides the "merit" aspect of meritocracy, there's the "-ocracy" aspect—the question of whether any society can successfully land on just the right criteria, and just the right selection method, so as to produce a truly wise, benign, unselfish elite. A sacred text for Conant and other promoters of the testing system was a letter that Thomas Jefferson wrote to John Adams in 1813, during their long, remarkable postpresidential correspondence. "There is a natural aristocracy among men," Jefferson wrote. "The grounds of this are virtue and talents. . . . There is also an artificial aristocracy founded on wealth and birth, without either virtue or talents. . . . The natural aristocracy I consider as the most precious gift of nature for the instruction, the trusts, and government of society."[3] The SAT was meant to bring what Jefferson had dreamed of into being, in an orderly, bureaucratized form.

Rarely quoted, though, is Adams's reply to Jefferson's letter, which was highly skeptical—indeed, sarcastic:

> Your distinction between natural and artificial Aristocracy does not appear to me well founded. Birth and Wealth are conferred on some Men, as imperiously by Nature, as Genius, Strength or Beauty. . . . And both artificial Aristocracy, and Monarchy, and civil, military, political and hierarchical despotism, have all grown out of the natural Aristocracy of "Virtues and Talents." We, to be sure, are far remote from this. Many hundred years must roll away before we shall be corrupted. Our pure, virtuous public spirited federative republic will last forever, govern the globe, and introduce the perfectibility of man. . . . Your distinction between the aristoi and pseudo aristoi, will not help the matter. I would

trust one as soon as the other with unlimited Power. The Law wisely refuses an Oath as a witness in his own cause to the Saint as well as to the Sinner.[4]

It's true that some vital roles in society require extensive technical education and training, but competent experts are not the same thing as a natural aristocracy that essentially rules, presumably without the inherent flaws of previous and supposedly unnatural aristocracies. Adams's warning was prescient, especially in light of the tendency of inheritance to play an ever-greater role in elite selection, once a set of criteria is established.

The founders of the American system of admissions testing were not cynical in their incessant use of rhetoric about democracy and opportunity. Indeed, their use of this rhetoric at the outset has been helpful to later efforts to make the system somewhat more fair. It would be more accurate to accuse them of being disingenuous and naive than cynical. They could be seen as disingenuous because Conant, especially, was overwhelmingly more interested in elite selection than in mass opportunity, and he took pains to disguise that in the way he presented his vision to the public. There is a big difference between democratic elite selection and true equal opportunity for all. They could be accused of being naive because Conant didn't see how impure both the "merit" and the "-ocracy" aspects of the system could become, rather quickly—the former because of the heavy aspect of status heritability among the privileged, the latter because of the association, especially in the United States, between selective higher education admission and pecuniary success, rather than public service.

(It surely would have disappointed Conant to see, all these years later, how few of the students admitted to the most elite undergraduate colleges spend their entire careers in government.) Conant predicted that private universities in the United States would disappear entirely. Instead, they remain the country's most prestigious, and the leading public universities have come to resemble the private ones in their heavy reliance on fundraising. Most of the country's leading scholars of poverty, inequality, and social stratification have chosen to locate themselves at these universities, and it's no mystery why: they have the resources to fund ambitious research and to attract brilliant graduate students, and they have the prestige to attract attention to their faculty members' work. The pull of the elite end of the system is nearly impossible to resist, for anyone who has access to it.

Recent American writers about meritocracy—from Charles Murray and Richard Herrnstein on the right to Daniel Markovitz or Michael Sandel on the left—have tended to agree with Young's premise that (in Murray and Herrnstein's phrase) a highly significant "invisible migration" has taken place in which, during the late twentieth century, very smart people were identified by standardized tests and brought to highly selective universities, where they replaced the previously dominant, not especially bright, class of boarding school aristocrats. This was not a change that would show up on national statistical surveys because it involved such a small number of people, and it did not even amount to a complete change in the population of elite universities, but it felt world-historically dramatic to the inhabitants of that small, intense world. Think, for example, of January 1993, when George and Barbara Bush, children of great privilege who had met at a country club dance in a wealthy suburb of New York City, turned over the White House to Bill and Hillary Clinton, who had grown up in middle-class provincial obscurity and who met in the library at Yale Law School. The new meritocratic elite inhabited the same institutions as the old aristocratic elite, and they began to take on the characteristics of a new kind of hereditary upper class, by intermarrying and raising their offspring with an obsessive concern with elite education.

One reason why the controversies over affirmative action have been so fierce for so long is that, structurally, the dreams of Conant, Clark Kerr, and likeminded mid-twentieth-century higher education leaders came true. The small number of highly selective American colleges and universities are for the most part more prominent, more successful, and further distanced from the great mass of schools than they were seventy-five years ago. They are highly overrepresented in the leadership ranks of many fields. If their goal has been to enhance their own institutional preeminence, they have succeeded magnificently; if their goal has been to create a fairer American society, not so much. In recent decades, research has generally supported the instincts of students and their parents who are applying to college: a degree from a highly selective university carries a significant lifetime earnings premium; the attention these universities pay to their students is far above average; their degrees carry valuable credential and network effects long after graduation; and their students come overwhelmingly from affluent families. Left to operate on its own, the system demonstrably underrepresents large elements of American society, and that affects not just campus diversity but who's in the room, and which perspectives are represented and respected, when consequential political and economic decisions are made for many years afterward. It's an issue obviously worth fighting over.

As part of the process that led to the University of California's elimination of standardized testing in admissions, the university's academic senate was invited to produce a report on testing. Anybody who assumes that University of California faculty members can be counted on to line up with the Left on all issues would be surprised by the report, which is a strong endorsement of the continued use of the SAT and ACT in admissions. (The university's board of regents, in eliminating testing, was rejecting the academic senate's recommendation.) The main argument of the senate's report is that the tests not only add to the predictive power of the high school transcript—they are actually slightly more predictive than grades. So why not use them? Saul Geiser immediately fired back after the report was issued, asserting that if you take the income and education levels of applicants' parents into account, it restores the superiority of high school grades to test scores as predictors of academic success. There is a larger issue here than who's right about predictive validity coefficients. The academic senate's report assumes that highly selective universities should choose their students primarily on their potential to perform academically on arrival at the university. But graduates of the University of California are, on the whole, likely to wind up in careers that are high status but not academic. It's the idea that the university is selecting a class of future leaders for a highly diverse state that widens the focus of admissions decisions beyond a sole concern with under-graduate academic performance.

Through all these decades of controversies about admissions and about affirmative action, there has been the idea, shimmering like the mirage of a desert oasis on the horizon, that there might be some way of selecting students for elite universities that everyone would agree is fair. It's the ever-elusive admissions equivalent of the Holy Grail, or the universal solvent, or the Northwest Passage. The main conservative version of this is to eliminate consideration of race in admissions. (And even the current Supreme Court is apparently not completely comfortable with the racial effects of strict "colorblindness"—that appears to explain its having declined in 2024 to hear a case challenging the admissions policies of a highly selective high school in Virginia, which substantively was almost identical to the 2023 Harvard and University of North Carolina cases.) Then there's the idea of eliminating the admissions preference for children of alumni—something that two unsuccessful presidential candidates over the years, Bob Dole and John Edwards, have proposed as federal legislation, and that three prominent colleges, Amherst, Johns Hopkins, and Wesleyan, have recently done. Preferences for athletes and for donors' children could also be eliminated.

Probably the most persistent reform idea is of a race-blind socioeconomic preference. Anthony Carnevale, when he was at ETS, produced a "Strivers Index," which would identify SAT takers who got scores significantly higher than one would have predicted from their socioeconomic background factors. Some years earlier another ETS psychometrician, Winton

Manning, proposed adjusting the SAT score itself to account for a student's socioeconomic background. Richard Kahlenberg, a policy analyst at the Century Foundation, has been advocating for class- rather than race-based affirmative action for decades, including in briefs he has filed in challenges to affirmative action that have come before the Supreme Court. (Even Kahlenberg, however, has endorsed race-conscious policies meant to integrate the student bodies of public schools rather than selective universities.) During the arguments before the Court in the most recent cases, several justices asked about the possibility of keeping affirmative action in admissions, but on the basis of class rather than race.

In October 2023, a few months after the Supreme Court decision banning race-based affirmative action in admissions, Opportunity Insights, a Harvard-based research institute directed by the economist Raj Chetty, issued a detailed report on admissions at the Ivy Plus schools—the most highly selective universities in the country. The report's headline finding was that students from families in the top 1 percent of the income distribution have a much higher chance of admission than anybody else, and that isn't because they have superior grades or test scores; the primary mechanisms by which their parents convert family money into admission are through the preferences for children of alumni and for athletes.[5] The obvious implication is that getting rid of these preferences would make superelite admissions—which, the study takes pains to stipulate, pays off handsomely in the form of access to high-paying private sector jobs—considerably fairer.

The study also showed that SAT scores are far more predictive of academic performance than high school grades—so it also seemed to argue for reinstituting SAT requirements, as several Ivy Plus schools did after the study was published.[6] Chetty and his coauthors, David Deming and John Friedman, avoided confronting what has always been the main issue about the SAT and admissions, which is the strong negative effect the test has on the Black presence at elite schools, by not presenting any data disaggregated by race. (Data from the College Board shows that in 2023, the gap between average Asian and Black scores on the SAT was more than 300 points, and that nationally fewer than 2,300 Black students get combined scores of 1400 or above, which is generally considered what a student needs to be admitted to an Ivy Plus school.[7]) Chetty and his coauthors' heavy emphasis on applicants from families in the top 1 percent also obscures the strong association between SAT scores and class. A chart that can be found in their supporting data shows that of currently enrolled students at Ivy Plus schools, the top 10 percent of the family income distribution accounts for 98 percent of the students with combined SAT scores of 1500 or above; Ivy Plus students from the bottom half of the income distribution with combined SAT scores of 1400 or higher account for only 1.2 percent of the total.[8] The idea that SAT requirements are the only way to find students from disadvantaged families who would do well at Ivy Plus schools doesn't take into account how few such students there are, not to mention what the racial effects of SAT requirements would be. It's best to understand the various alternatives to affirmative action as testaments to the insolubility of the problem of selective college admissions, and of meritocracy more broadly—not to how easy the current system would be to fix. Most of the highly selective private universities have kept their preferences for the children of alumni and do-nors and for athletes for fundraising reasons, but it's also the case that because these applicants often come from privileged backgrounds, they are not obviously less academically credentialed than the overall applicant pool. Applicants from less advantaged backgrounds already receive informal preference at selective colleges, but if one is primarily concerned about the fairness of the system to each individual applicant, this practice doesn't pass the test because it necessarily entails denying a place to someone with superior credentials and giving it to someone else for social-justice reasons. The battle over affirmative action really boils down to whether race is the one and only offensive admissions preference out of all the preferences.

Selective admissions is a zero-sum game that gets ever more severe. Everything about making college admissions a highly consequential socioeconomic choke point generally favors students from fortunate backgrounds. It might help make selective college admissions fairer if (in the manner of many elite admissions systems in other countries) we had a national curriculum and a national system of public school funding, and if we imposed some kind of service requirement on selective university graduates so that admissions didn't so much resemble a ticket to private-sector success. But none of that is going to happen in the foreseeable future.

What if we imagined ourselves to be in the position Conant was in nearly a century ago, and gave ourselves the project of designing a national testing system to help manage the transition between high school and college—what would we do? The situation today is radically different from what it was then, and not only because the United States is both more diverse and more conscious of diversity as a goal. Today, 90 percent of Americans finish high school and have some interaction with the higher education system. The idea that there is a cohort of people of very high academic ability who will never enter a college or university no longer applies, though many people from disadvantaged backgrounds aim lower than they should and face severe financial and logistical obstacles as they enter the higher education system. The idea that elite universities have no reliable means of evaluating applicants who didn't go to a small handful of elite high schools no longer applies either. Standardized testing, of many kinds, pervades American public education. And highly selective universities have decades of experience in evaluating the high school records of students from a wide variety of institutions. There isn't the same sense of uncertainty that was part of what led Conant to embrace the SAT.

More fundamentally, the question of who should get the slots in highly selective colleges and universities, besides being very difficult to settle, is not the primary issue in American higher education, especially from the point of view of enhancing democracy and opportunity in America. It gets far more attention than it deserves. Only about 1 percent of American undergraduates attend the twenty-five or so colleges that accept fewer than 10 percent of their applicants. Only 3 percent attend the fifty or so colleges that accept fewer than 25 percent of their applicants. The selectivity of admission to college is not a major factor in the lives of the overwhelming majority of young Americans. The widespread administration of the SAT to millions of people in order to identify a relative handful to admissions officers at highly selective colleges, as if it were the glass slipper used to find Cinderella after the ball, creates the impression that it is more consequential to most test takers than it actually is.

The most obvious problem in American higher education today is not its inability to identify and educate top academic performers but its failure to produce a more widely successful experience for most students. Only about 40 percent of entering students get a bachelor's degree in four years, and only about 60 percent in six years. At community colleges, only about 30 percent of entering students complete a two-year degree program within three years. Completion rates are lower for Black and Latino students than for white and Asian students, lower for low-income students than for middle-class and affluent students, and lower for men than for women. At the same time, despite mythology to the contrary, completing a degree pays off. A 2021 study by Anthony Carnevale, Ban Cheah, and Emma Wenzinger of Georgetown University found that completing high school increases a person's lifetime earnings by 33 percent. A two-year associate's degree adds 25 percent to lifetime earnings over a high school diploma, and a four-year degree adds 75 percent to lifetime earnings. Graduate degrees add even more.[9] The study takes pains to point out that the return to higher education varies significantly by field of study; Carnevale and his colleagues have been strong advocates for a "return on investment" approach to higher education degrees that entails disaggregating the economic payoff by academic major. Their unsurprising finding is that business, engineering, mathematics, and computer science majors earn far more than the general run of graduates. Overall, though, completing a higher education degree is about the surest way for a young person to get on the path to a better future. Conversely, the current low degree completion rate is a glaring gap in the American opportunity structure, and bringing it higher ought to be an urgent national priority.

The United States made an idealistic bet on universal elementary education in the nineteenth century, and a similar bet on universal high school education in the early twentieth century, and a similar bet on universal higher education in the late twentieth century. At each stage there were skeptics who warned that the country was trying to educate the uneducable. Today, a good way into the twenty-first century, our progress in this long-running project of demonstrating a commitment to ordinary people's potential has stalled, because the massive higher education system we have built is not delivering the results it should for so many of its students. The great bulk of higher education takes place in unselective or minimally selective institutions, mainly in the public sector. What would most enhance opportunity for most Americans would be a successful passage through these institutions.

Could testing serve as an aid in that project? Yes, potentially, if it were testing of a different kind from what we have become accustomed to over all these years. The system of higher education testing built around the SAT and similar tests—aptitude tests aimed at selection—was not designed with the primary aim of distributing educational opportunity widely. At the time when the system was introduced there were other, competing ideas about what the main focus of American higher education should be, and their advocates had quite different kinds of tests, built for different purposes, in mind.

Testing is, of course, ubiquitous in education at all levels—it's almost impossible to imagine schools without both formative tests (like quizzes) and summative tests (like final exams). And there have always been voices in the never-ending debates about education that express an instinctive suspicion of all forms of testing, for the way they emphasize mastering material, rather than creativity and independent thinking, as a central purpose of schooling. For our purposes here, the question is whether tests that are made to be widely usable outside the confines of a single course at a single school could serve the aim of increasing educational opportunity broadly, for most people rather than for a lucky few, and in particular whether they could help to increase degree completion rates at community colleges and public universities.

In the 1951 book *Educational Measurement*, assembled by George Zook of the American Council on Education and E. F. Lindquist of the University of Iowa, the assumption running through all the chapters is that the one and only appropriate purpose of standardized testing is to enhance student learning as broadly as possible. (And indeed, that was also Alfred Binet's assumption back in 1905—it's a long-running tradition.) Testing is meant to help teachers teach their students more effectively, and therefore to help students achieve more in school. The testing pioneer Ralph Tyler, of the University of Chicago, in his contribution to *Educational Measurement*, defined teaching this way: "Basically, instruction is the process by which desirable changes are made in the behavior of students, using 'behavior' in the broad sense to include thinking, feeling, and acting. Instruction is not effective, therefore, unless some changes in the behavior of students have actually taken place."[10]

You can see from this what the appeal of standardized tests would be. Most of the contributors to *Educational Measurement* believed in the importance of what we'd now call learning outcomes: they were frustrated by the way students were being passed along in the education system merely by completing course material, and tested mainly on their mastery of sets of facts rather than the ability to think. New tests would help teachers to define their higher aims more precisely and to impart them to students in ways that would be profoundly helpful over the long term. For a student, not doing well on a test would open the way to extra educational opportunity—more intense teaching, toward a focused and meaningful educational goal—rather than signaling a limitation of opportunities.

In Richard Atkinson's critique of the SAT, which came after half a century of testing developments that weren't particularly well aligned with the vision of *Educational Measurement*, he highlighted a series of distinctions in testing that are important to keep in mind and are often ignored in testing debates that tend to treat tests as either all good or all bad. A standardized test can be designed for diagnosis or for prediction. The SAT is a predictive test, meant to forecast academic performance in college. A diagnostic test is meant to gauge a student's level of prior learning—for example, to help determine what level of course in a subject the student should take in college—and to identify areas where the student may need special help. A related distinction is the familiar one between an achievement test and an aptitude test. An aptitude test is designed to measure general-purpose academic ability. (Although the College Board and ETS have always stoutly insisted that SAT scores are used only in college admissions, and even there only cautiously, some employers that prize braininess, like hedge funds and technology companies, regularly ask job applicants for their SAT scores, if the applicants haven't already listed their scores on their résumés.) An achievement test measures mastery of a subject. For an achievement test, test prep and studying the course material should be the same thing; for an aptitude test, studying is supposed to be unnecessary, so test prep is the only available form of homework. A final distinction is between norm-referenced and criterion-referenced testing. A norm-referenced test (and again, the SAT is an example) measures where each test taker stands within the total pool of test takers, so as to let college admissions officers aim for, say, the top 5 percent of all scorers on the test. A criterion-referenced test measures a student's understanding of a specific body of material, so that the student is not compared with other students. In the proverbial elementary school weekly spelling test, in theory all the students could get perfect scores, because it's a criterion-referenced test.[11]

The SAT—a predictive test, an aptitude test, and a norm-referenced test—was designed to help elite colleges select a small handful of students. The reason it was designed to do that was that higher education leaders like Conant were trying to make their institutions more academic and to locate talent they believed they would otherwise miss. It wound up having a far broader effect, because of its use by many more colleges and universities than the original group, and because of its large impact on the high school experience of millions of students who don't go to highly selective colleges, in addition to the thousands who will. If, today, we define the problem that testing is meant to solve not as improving selection for a few elite universities but as improving the too-low graduation rates and other aspects of the student learning experience at a large number of relatively unselective universities, we would be drawn to diagnostic rather than predictive tests, to achievement rather than aptitude tests, and to criterion-referenced rather than norm-referenced tests. And these, in order to serve the purpose they are meant to serve, would have to go along with larger structural changes: a much greater emphasis on teaching and advising in higher education, and a strengthening of the curriculum in high school. This ought to be a national project on the scale of the project that brought us the current higher education admissions system, or on an even grander scale.

It looks as if the college admissions tests that have been widely in place since the Second World War may be on their way out, except perhaps at a small number of highly selective schools. Fundamentally, that isn't a sign that the country has "turned against meritocracy," but that the tests, rather than representing an opposing force to the existing class system, by now, on the whole, reinforce it. One sometimes hears lamentations that, if the many colleges and universities that have suspended them don't resume their use, it will signal a wholesale abandonment of academic standards, or of the principle of meritocratic admissions. Those fears are wildly overblown. Elite colleges and universities are overwhelmingly academic institutions, where the high school record is the most important admissions criterion for applicants, and published academic research is almost the only criterion for the hiring and promotion of faculty. Because the standardized admissions tests pick up so much family background, the number of students who come from disadvantaged back-grounds and who went to underperforming high schools but who nevertheless get superior scores on standardized tests is tiny. It's not worth designing a whole system just to catch a handful of people who, in the twenty-first century, will be going to college anyway. It would be far better to expend the country's energies on making the higher education system work better for the great bulk of students than on fiercely debating what amount to incremental adjustments in the apportionment of a highly limited number of spaces in highly selective institutions.

The most useful next national educational project would be to focus on the broad end of the educational system, not the narrow end—to try to create through education as much meaningful opportunity for flourishing for as many people as possible. Testing could serve that project, if it were a quite different kind of testing, but the project shouldn't be thought of as being mainly about testing. It would mainly be about adopting a different set of primary educational and social goals.

Given the history of testing, a measure of wariness about its widespread use is justified. Tests can take on a life of their own. They can be seen as measures of immutable traits, rather than as snapshots of students' achievement at a moment in time—something that is highly mutable. They can be used to reduce educational opportunity rather than enhance it, and to disempower teachers rather than enable them to help their students learn more effectively. Because tests themselves are so visible and the purposes behind them are far less so, it's possible, unless we're vigilant, for the ongoing widespread use of testing to hide quite radical shifts in the social and educational ideas underlying them.

But it's worth imagining the good that tests could do. They could give schools and teachers a better idea of exactly where a student is at the moment, which would permit a more effective, tailored approach to that student's instruction. They could offer a sense of a student's overall strengths and weaknesses that might shape future educational choices. They could assess a student's level of knowledge of a body of material that has to be learned. They could serve as a check on students' and teachers' self-reports of how well the students are learning. All of these purposes have deep roots in the history of testing—deeper, in fact, than testing for selective admissions. The essential question is not whether to have tests; it's what broad educational goals tests should serve.

What should those goals be? Every American child should have a decent public education that leaves him or her truly literate, numerate, and able to think and act as an empowered citizen. To accomplish that would require significantly reforming the school system so that the all-poor, usually all-minority, severely underresourced schools that occupy the system's bottom tier would become much better. After high school, we would direct the same passion, commitment, and resources to community colleges and less selective public colleges and universities, in order to enhance learning and increase completion rates. Such changes would surely not eliminate corrosive inequality in the United States, but they would provide far more opportunity to far more people. It's impossible to retrofit a system designed around the elite into a system that serves the interests of most people.

Americans love the ideal of equal opportunity for all. As a vehicle for that idea, admission to highly selective colleges and universities is unworkable almost by definition, because people with advantages so powerfully don't want their own children to forgo those advantages, but if we want to come closer to the ideal, we should recognize that operating a series of highly consequential education selections works against it. Early in life, people are most likely to be products of their backgrounds rather than of their own efforts. The more that life-determining decisions can be pushed back into adulthood, rather than taking place during childhood and adolescence, the fairer and more democratic the system will be. The more success can depend on demonstrated performance at work, rather than assumed potential determined by academic measures, the fairer and more democratic the system will be. The more it is accepted that individual status and success may fluctuate over the course of a person's life, rather than being locked in at a relatively early age, the fairer and more democratic the system will be. Accomplishing all this depends on our seeing the fundamental purpose of education as being to equip as many people as possible for as broad a set of life circumstances as possible.

The idea of a test-based meritocracy rests on the assumption that one of the core purposes of education is to designate a limited cohort of winners relatively early in their lives. If you object to that, what you're really objecting to is the assumption, not the tests used to instantiate it. Whether or not the familiar higher education admissions tests go away, real change will require that Americans learn to focus not on tests, and not on elite selection, but on how well our educational system works for most people. Doing that will require breaking some deeply ingrained bad habits that reside in all of us, like the habit of being unable to direct our primary attention to the lives lived by most people, rather than those lived by a small cohort of the anointed. Just as it's an illusion to believe that standardized admissions tests for highly selective colleges represent opportunity in America, it's also an illusion to believe that dropping these tests would bring about the dawn of a new age of truly meaningful equal opportunity in America. That will be a different project, much larger, and far more important.

Higher Admissions, a California Perspective

Patricia Gándara

IN *HIGHER ADMISSIONS: The Rise, Decline, and Return of Standardized Testing,* Nicholas Lemann takes on what he has referred to as "the big test" and traces the trajectory of the SAT from its relatively benign—even almost democratic—origins to its establishment as the arbiter of merit or academic worthiness in higher education. Designed as an aptitude test to identify talented young men who weren't from the same elite schools that typically produced the student body at Harvard and other Ivy League schools, the SAT cracked open the door for a few, but slammed it shut for many others. It also evolved from its origins in early tests of intelligence to be a predictor of achievement in college (at least in the first year), purposely eschewing the term "aptitude." Nonetheless these test scores have come to define academic promise and have played what some consider an outsize role in distributing opportunity in

TABLE 1. Average SAT scores by race or ethnicity and first language, California high school graduates, 2019

Race or ethnicity	Average score
Asian	1,214
White	1,168
Latino	976
Black	948
Native American	950
English not first language	1,036

Source: College Board, SAT participation and performance, 2019.

higher education. As the American population diversified and more students from disadvantaged and "minority" groups headed off for college and were compelled to take the test, it became clear that there were vast differences in these students' performance by background. See table 1, for example.

The reader may not be surprised by these score gaps among different racial and ethnic groups, as they are widely discussed in the popular press. However, many people would likely be surprised to learn that the relative order of scores by race and ethnicity is the same or similar for almost *any standardized test* given: Asian, white, Latino, Black, in that order. First language is rarely mentioned as a factor in testing outcomes, but it plays a significant role as well. As long as test takers are compared against each other (as in norm-referenced tests), the relative order of scores will almost always be the same. Asian and white students receive higher scores, and Black and Latino students receive lower scores.

Standardization itself is often invoked as the culprit for these disparities in test scores. The view is that if only we refrained from the use of standardized tests, we could better address the problem of inequalities in educational outcomes. But "standardized" simply means everyone gets the same content and conditions of test administration. In fact, notwithstanding the criticism often leveled against standardized tests as being unfair for some groups, standardization is considered by test makers to be the hallmark of good practice in assessment. It is defined by the 2014 *ETS Standards for Quality and Fairness* as "the aspects of the test and testing environment that are required to be the same for most test takers, to allow fair comparison of their scores."[1] It has generally been viewed as bad practice to compare students on different material or under different circumstances, although some researchers are beginning to question this belief. Randy Bennett at ETS, and some others, are asking the question, If students have vastly different experiences and attend schools with vastly different resources, is it fair to give them all the same test? Bennett is researching the possibilities for tests or assessments that are personalized to students from diverse backgrounds and take advantage of their unique experiences, knowledge, and skills. But this work is inordinately complicated and only at the beginning stages. In the meantime, standardization remains.

Using high school grades instead of test scores does not solve the problem of preordained rankings either. GPAs follow the same patterns as standardized tests. Asian, white, and upper-income students have, on average, higher GPAs than Black, Latino, and lower-income students. Lemann argues that other kinds of tests—not norm referenced—should be considered to avoid the tyranny of the standardized test scores. But these alternatives have their drawbacks as well. For example, AP courses taken and tests passed are also used as ways to distinguish among students for high-stakes purposes, but these courses are not equally distributed among schools, nor is the quality of instruction. Schools that serve low-income and minority students tend to offer fewer AP courses, and those that are offered are often taught by less experienced teachers. As such, less advantaged students take fewer AP courses and pass the AP tests at lower rates. This pattern of differences is not due to differences in natural ability, or even to differences in effort. It is due to vast differences in background factors such as parental education and immigrant status, socioeconomic status, and, importantly, the quality of schooling that students receive—things over which students have little to no control.

Acknowledging this fact, in 1999 Anthony Carnevale at ETS proposed what he called the Strivers Index, contextualizing SAT scores by applying students' socioeconomic background and schooling factors to interpretation of their test scores. In other words, the scores of students from disadvantaged circumstances could be viewed in a context that presumably reflected their capabilities notwithstanding their disadvantaged backgrounds. This met with a firestorm of criticism and was quickly shelved. Two decades later, the College Board released its Landscape system, which attempted to do something similar, taking into account neighborhood and schooling factors that were known to correlate with test scores. It was introduced rather quietly as something that could assist higher education institutions in their admissions decisions, but it was purely optional. It faced a similar outcry as the Strivers Index and has not been widely promoted. Both of these efforts have been an attempt to acknowledge—and address—the elephant in the room: students from different racial and socioeconomic backgrounds perform differently on these tests through no fault (or lack of effort) of their own, and this can have major consequences for their futures and equality of opportunity more generally. But the test scores are reified in the minds of many people as representing something innate in the individual, not to be tampered with by adjusting scores: they define merit.

Given that the tests are so problematic, why are we, as a society, so committed to testing generally, and more specifically in the case of college admissions? The question of whether and how to utilize the SAT (and ACT) was posed to the University of California in 2019 by the then-president Janet Napolitano. A task force was formed of faculty from across the ten-campus system to study the issue. This was named the Standardized Testing Task Force and was given until January 2020 to complete the study. I served on that task force and helped to write the report. Although it was reported that the task force "unanimously" supported the recommendation to continue the use of the tests, this was not quite true. There was considerable debate about their use. On the side of continued use were primarily the arguments that the test enhanced—however modestly—the predictiveness of how students would perform early in their college careers and that there was some evidence that "diamonds in the rough" (students who had not performed particularly well in high school but showed great promise on the test) were uncovered. It had also been noted by admissions officers that since the University of California received so many more qualified applicants than seats available, they needed all the data they could get to make difficult decisions, and in any case the test scores were only one of many factors considered.

On the side of reconsidering the use of the tests was the fundamental inequity of using a test that was known to disadvantage underrepresented students, who were nearly two-thirds of the state's high school graduates but who were seriously underrepresented in the university. Moreover, although it was contended that the test scores contributed only modestly to the final decision, the weight they are given in peoples' perceptions could not be overlooked, and once seen, the scores could not be unseen. But two other points were raised that were too easily dismissed. First, the predictive power of the test was based on the assumption that there would be no support for students whose test scores were lower but whose promise was high (the opposite of the "diamonds in the rough" whose test scores were high but actual school performance was not): effectively, the good students who came from poor schools or very limited circumstances. Second, most Black and Latino students did not have the resources to prepare for the test, while their more advantaged peers had access to test prep courses and even expensive coaches who worked with them one-on-one. These students were also acutely aware that students from their background tended to score much lower than others, and many no doubt failed to even apply to the university for fear of being rejected. We had reason to believe that this might be true.

In a small study we conducted with about fifty high-achieving Latino students seeking a college scholarship,[2] we found that, *independent of high school GPA*, students who scored lower on the SAT also tended to perceive themselves as less able than students with higher SAT scores. Some of these high-performing students admitted that the test scores surprised them and made them wonder if they really were capable of achieving their academic goals. Perhaps most important, but least discussed, is the way that a test score can affect students' perceptions of their abilities. The doubt that is engendered by a low test score can result in a reluctance to even apply for a school or program in which they fear they cannot succeed. When bright students are dissuaded by a low test score from applying to a selective college, they reduce their chances of completing a degree. Research is clear: the more selective the college, the greater are the chances of degree completion. Moreover, when these students take themselves out of the running, they reduce the racial and socioeconomic diversity of the more selective institutions, which denies everyone a richer education.

In fact, after the SAT was removed from the application process by the regents of the University of California (in contradiction to the task force recommendation), the numbers of applicants from underrepresented groups rose significantly, as did the numbers of students admitted from those groups. For example, Black freshman applicants rose by about 48 percent at both the University of California, Los Angeles, and the University of California, Berkeley, and Latino applicants increased by 33 percent at UCLA and 36 percent at Berkeley. This resulted in historically high rates of admission for these groups. University of California campus officials credited the gains to the elimination of standardized testing requirements.[3] The fear of failure generated by the test, which was no longer required, apparently had been a factor in reducing applications from underrepresented students, thus affecting their representation in the university. Interestingly, the lack of test scores did not seem to affect the selection process, even though admissions officers were given very little time to adapt to the new rules. The university relied on thirteen other factors, including things like overcoming challenges, having developed special talents, and receiving achievements and awards, to distinguish among similarly strong students.

Given the debacle in California and the declining numbers of colleges and universities requiring the test, Lemann predicts that the test is on its way out, which he contends is a good thing. And yet, the 2023 Supreme Court decision in *Students for Fair Admissions v. Harvard* (and University of North Carolina) to bar the use of affirmative action in college admissions may complicate the matter. Anti–affirmative action forces may want to lobby for the use of the test in admissions, as it has been invoked repeatedly in the arguments against positive consideration of race. Quantitative measures—test scores—are viewed by many as more reliable, less biased, and more reflective of inherent ability than nonquantifiable characteristics such as "grit" or motivation. In terms of fairness, and possibly utility, this no doubt makes a certain amount of sense. But there are challenges inherent in all kinds of tests, as there are with the SAT. Would changing the way we assess students fundamentally change the problems associated with standardized test scores? Could a high score on a standardized achievement test instead of an SAT score become the new arbiter of merit? Would it result in different winners or losers?

The evidence suggests not. Many people worry that this would just create a new "arms race" around these tests, with the same kind of test prep that raises equity questions about the SAT.

Alternatives to the Meritocracy of the SAT

In place of tests such as the SAT, Lemann recommends different kinds of tests—diagnostic tests, presumably to help educators improve students' learning, rather than predictive tests; achievement tests that provide evidence of what a student knows, rather than aptitude tests that presume to predict future learning; and criterion-referenced tests to determine whether the student has met a particular standard, rather than norm-referenced tests that measure test takers against each other. While seemingly more benign than the SAT, these alternative tests have their own limitations.

For selective colleges, diagnostic tests provide little information to help make difficult admissions decisions or determine who will win a scholarship competition. For most colleges, however, they could be a resource to help students improve academically, but to be useful they need to be paired with academic supports, which can be costly and therefore work against students' admission. Diagnostic testing is generally done to determine how a person learns or whether a person has some impediment to learning. It is often done in one-on-one settings by a specialist, but some forms of diagnostic testing can be administered in groups, such as with formative assessments where students are tested periodically to track their progress. However, in survey after survey teachers claim that their own homemade tests are often more useful, and timely, for understanding how their students are faring than off-the-shelf tests. It must be borne in mind also that diagnostic testing leads to diagnoses, which run the risk of being stigmatizing or resulting in undesirable outcomes such as academic tracking, which can limit access to college preparatory curricula.

Some have argued for substituting the SAT with achievement test scores, but this would produce similarly unequal outcomes by race and class. The most ubiquitous testing is the achievement tests required by state and federal departments of education to track schools' progress toward meeting educational goals. These tests are designed to determine how groups of students and schools are faring academically. Although these tests take up a considerable amount of instructional time, both to prepare for them and to administer them, and the outcomes of these tests rarely are available in time to alter instruction, they are generally acknowledged as being necessary to hold schools accountable. In spite of parents' desire to know how their own children are performing vis-à-vis a standard, most accountability tests are not designed to provide detailed information about individual students. Given the general frustration with too much testing, it is doubtful that much support could be garnered for additional achievement testing.

There is also a pernicious side to widespread achievement testing such as that required for accountability. These scores routinely undermine school integration—a key source of the inequalities that exist in American society. Even good schools with strong teachers that enroll lower-income students or students of color are likely to score lower on standardized tests and struggle to attract a more diverse population. Realtors often steer home buyers and renters toward neighborhood schools with high test scores, which tend to be more white and socioeconomically advantaged. Real estate values are thus driven in part by neighborhood school test scores, which can also affect the tax base for these struggling schools. This creates a challenge for educators trying to integrate the schools and provide a high-quality education for all students.

Criterion-referenced testing is used where it is important to know whether a student or a class has met a given standard and where comparison to other students is not an issue. Criterion-referenced tests may also be used to determine whether candidates meet particular qualifications for a program, a job, or some other benefit, but they do not provide information about what students are actually capable of, what level they should aspire to, or the level at which the "average" student is performing. They are of very little use in comparing students for any purpose, and comparative information, too, can be important for informing and individualizing instruction.

Why Do We Test?

Given the problems with all kinds of tests, is there a real alternative? Whether students are tested with something like the SAT or simply with achievement tests—criterion referenced or not—the outcomes may be similar if the distribution of resources in society remain so unequal. Considering the high correlation between test scores and socioeconomic status and the consistent distribution of scores with Asians at the high end, followed by white, Latino, and Black students, the tests are a way to maintain privilege for many. Perhaps the best that can be done is to eschew the tests altogether, at least for the purposes of distributing opportunity. Admitting the top x percent[4] of students from each high school based on GPA is one alternative. It worked reasonably well in Texas as long as it was paired with additional support and the schools remained segregated, with the lower-income students and students of color enrolled in the same (often inferior) schools. It also reduced the University of Texas's degrees of freedom in admissions as more and more students came into the university through this avenue. Clearly this was trading one kind of disadvantage for another. In California a similar plan targeting the top 9 percent has continued to operate, but it has tended to capture pretty much the same students the university system was already admitting through other means.

The University of California's comprehensive review of thirteen factors is another option. It is hugely labor intensive and requires considerable training and resources, but it may be the most equitable of available options. The thirteen factors considered in application reviews (initially fourteen factors, until the SAT was removed) include several related to academic programs such as GPA and numbers of advanced courses taken and passed. But several factors that are nonquantitative include special talents, achievements and awards,[5] participation in educational preparation programs, academic accomplishment in light of life experiences, and geographic location. In this context the meritocracy is based on a compilation of human characteristics that better reflect the totality of the person and what they have to contribute to the university and the society.

Of course, some students always have an advantage, as their schools and their families can provide experiences, opportunities, and even the time to engage in these things that low-income parents cannot. It's much easier to excel in the arts or devote time to community service if you don't have an after-school job to help support the family or need to care for younger siblings. A professional parent has many more contacts to provide interesting opportunities for their children than parents who must work two or three jobs that offer no autonomy or contact with individuals with significant social capital.

As long as we live in an egregiously unequal society, it is probably impossible to create an assessment system that treats all students equally, but moving in the direction of assessment that considers the whole person, including their background and experiences as well as their cultural and linguistic strengths, can probably bring us closer to that goal and hopefully dispel the myth of test score meritocracy.

Alternatively, given that meritocracy is itself a social construction, it can be redefined in any way we choose. If universities defined their role as reducing social and economic inequality, meritocracy could mean offering the best educational opportunities most broadly to the greatest diversity of students, especially those from lower-income circumstances. As Rebecca Zwick notes, quoting from Sen (2000), "conventional notions of 'meritocracy' often attach the label of merit to *people*," but the designation should instead be applied to *actions*. An action is meritocratic if it promotes a valued societal goal."[6]

Meritocracy might then be defined by characteristics that hold the greatest promise for contributing to the common good. Rather than a high test score, students would be offered admission based on their unique talents, experiences, and goals that contributed to creating a more equitable society. To some extent, the University of California's thirteen factors represent an attempt to balance between the personal and the social good in admissions decisions.

The Future of the Meritocracy

Marvin Krislov

NICHOLAS LEMANN says the meritocracy has always been a fraud.

Even the term itself isn't quite on the level, as he notes in his compelling and very informative book. The British sociologist Michael Young, writing in the 1950s, settled on the label when he was looking for a word to describe a society led by those who'd earned their position through education, intelligence, and hard work, rather than by accident of birth.[1] The problem is that Young picked a Latin prefix with an identical meaning to that of the Greek prefix in the term already in use. In other words, Lemann explains, etymologically speaking, "meritocracy" and "aristocracy" are *both* "rule by the best." They mean the same thing.

Nomenclature aside, the concept has had other problems from the beginning, too. Lemann opens his book by highlighting the very deep roots of some modern objections to perhaps

the chief organizing metric of the modern American meritocracy, the SAT. It turns out it has been dismissed by some nearly
since its inception. As early as 1948, academics at the University of Chicago labeled intelligence tests fraudulent, vehicles
for, as Lemann writes in a critique that stands up well today,
"wrapping the fortunate children of the middle and upper
classes in a mantle of scientifically demonstrated superiority."
Lemann reports that even earlier, in 1932, the man who'd
invented the SAT, Carl Brigham, an early advocate for intelligence tests and not coincidentally once an ardent eugenicist,
fully recanted his views on all those matters in the book *A
Study of Error*.

But eye-opening as Lemann's historical study is, it is arguably superfluous. There is plenty of evidence all around
us that the meritocracy, as currently constructed, is not
working. A study released in the summer of 2023 by Opportunity Insights, a group of academic economists studying
inequality, found that the children of the rich are far overrepresented at the so-called Ivy Plus colleges, which are the
eight members of the Ivy League plus CalTech, the University of Chicago, Duke, Georgetown, Johns Hopkins, MIT,
Northwestern, Rice, Stanford, and Washington University
(Missouri). "For applicants with the same SAT or ACT score,
children from families in the top 1 percent were 34 percent
more likely to be admitted than the average applicant, and
those from the top 0.1 percent were more than twice as likely
to get in," as the *New York Times* wrote in its coverage of the
report.[2]

Indeed, it is worth quoting at length from the Opportunity
Insights study itself, because it is such a clear indictment of the

purported ideals of our meritocracy. Here is just part of its introduction:

> Leadership positions in the United States are held dispro-portionately by graduates of a small number of highly se-lective private colleges. Less than half of one percent of Americans attend Ivy-Plus college. . . . Yet these twelve colleges account for more than 10% of Fortune 500 CEOs, a quarter of U.S. Senators, half of all Rhodes scholars, and three-fourths of Supreme Court justices appointed in the last half-century. . . . Ivy-Plus colleges also enroll a dispro-portionate share of students from high-income families: students from families in the top 1% of the income distribu-tion are more than twice as likely to attend an Ivy-Plus col-lege than students with comparable SAT or ACT scores from the middle class. . . .
>
> Two-thirds of the difference in enrollment rates at Ivy-Plus colleges by parental income can be explained by higher *admissions* rates for students from high-income families. Conditional on SAT/ACT scores, applicants from families in the top 1% (incomes > $611,000) are 58% more likely to be admitted to Ivy-Plus colleges than applicants from middle-class families, which we define in this study as those with parental incomes between the 70th and 80th percen-tiles of the national income distribution ($91,000–$114,000), roughly the middle decile of the parental income distribution for applicants to highly selective colleges. . . .
>
> . . . 24% of the admissions advantage for students from top 1% families can be explained by the recruitment of athletes, who tend to come from higher-income families.

Another 46% of the admissions advantage comes from preferential admission for students whose parents attended the same college ("legacies"). This is both because legacy students are disproportionately likely to come from families in the top 1% and because the legacy advantage is particularly large among high-income families. Legacy students from families in the top 1% are 5 times as likely to be admitted as the average applicant with similar test scores, demographic characteristics, and admissions office ratings; legacy students from families below the 90th percentile are 3 times as likely to be admitted as peers with comparable credentials. . . .

The remaining 31% of the admissions advantage for students from families in the top 1% is explained by the fact that they are judged to have stronger non-academic credentials (e.g., extracurricular activities, leadership traits, etc.) than students from lower-income families.[3]

To put it even more succinctly: For elite jobs, it helps a lot to have gone to elite schools. (The first paragraph of the Opportunity Insights introduction limits itself to data on CEOs and senators, but the reality is that even to get a just-out-of-college foot in the door at a Goldman Sachs or a Google, all signs suggest the same schools are prerequisites to entry.) And your chances of getting into an elite school are much greater if your parents are wealthy. We know wealth helps because admissions tools like the SAT favor the wealthy, but Opportunity Insights found that *even controlling for SAT scores*, the wealthy are more likely to be admitted, because they're more likely to be athletes, more likely to be legacies, and more likely to have better nonacademic credentials like extracurricular activities and leadership traits.

Even when everything else is equal, which it never is, the kids of the wealthy are the ones who have the time and resources to do the things that give them great college applications: they can volunteer with the organization that builds their leadership skills, they can spend summers working as unpaid interns to try out the careers they might be interested in, and they can go on that spring break trip to rebuild houses after the hurricane in the Caribbean.

In 2017, Brookings Institution scholar Richard V. Reeves published *Dream Hoarders: How the American Upper Middle Class Is Leaving Everyone Else in the Dust, Why That Is a Problem, and What to Do about It*. In it, he examined the status anxiety of the American upper-middle class and the ways members of that class jealously guard its privileges for their children. The American Dream is social mobility—but it is human nature to want that mobility to only move one way. "Every college place or internship that goes to one of our kids because of a legacy bias or personal connection is one less available to others," he writes.[4] He devotes the bulk of the book to finding ways to unlock the hoarding.

He's against legacy admissions, and he sees the kinds of unpaid internships that help kids prepare for college as a boondoggle. He quotes another commentator who wrote that unpaid internships "aren't morally defensible." But he believes that simply abolishing them would be too draconian. He argues for resetting our standards. "Right now," he writes, "Americans are literally shameless about the way they hand out and take up internships." But he is hopeful for change, and quotes the New York University philosopher Samuel Scheffler: "Behavior that is seen in one social setting as an admirable expression of parental concern may be seen in another as an intolerable form of favoritism or nepotism."[5]

From where I sit, that reset couldn't happen soon enough.

That our meritocracy has in many ways turned into an aristocracy isn't just bad for the American ideal and for the millions of Americans who are locked out of the opportunities from which they could benefit; it's not helping America to succeed in the increasingly competitive global marketplace.

As we have seen, the children of the elite are getting ahead in this country—dominating our elite schools, running our elite institutions—not necessarily because they're best qualified to do so but because the system is stacked to allow them to do so. In reality, it simply cannot be the case that all the talent in America happens to overlap with those whose parents control the most wealth. It simply cannot be that the most intellect and brain power lie with those who happen to take up the sports most in demand on Ivy League campuses, or that the most creativity and the best new ideas belong to those whose parents also attended those schools. To the contrary, imagine the talent we could have access to, the ideas and perspectives and energy and creativity we could unlock, when we finally unleash the power of all those young people who haven't grown up already within the dream, to use Reeves's metaphor.

For the sake of those young people, and for the sake of leveraging their insights and talents as we seek to ensure that America can compete and thrive in a multipolar twenty-first century, a successful meritocracy must remain our goal. The idea that the right combination of intelligence, ambition, and effort—merit, you might say—can lead anyone to the highest levels of success, if they're just willing to put in the work, is a noble one, however troubled its history or flawed its previous execution.

Our challenge is to find a way to live up to that paradigm.

In part, it's what nearly a half century of affirmative action attempted to accomplish. As Lemann's history describes, through the bulk of the latter half of the twentieth century, the American public and the American higher education establishment were simultaneously committed to two ideals, or at least said they were: meritocracy and integration. But the reality of systemic, legalized discrimination until at least the mid-1960s, and persistent wealth and opportunity imbalances thereafter, left those two goals sitting uneasily side by side.

From the *Bakke* decision in 1978, which confirmed that schools have a "compelling interest" in a diverse student body and disallowed quotas but permitted affirmative action on what was then termed the Harvard model, which considered race as one factor among many; through the Michigan cases in 2003, in which I was deeply involved, which confirmed diversity as a state interest and affirmed the constitutionality of considering race in admissions, so long as it was considered in a "narrowly tailored" and individualized way; and then the Texas cases in 2013 and 2016, which reaffirmed the Michigan ruling, affirmative action was a limited attempt to find a way to make the meritocracy achieve the goals it is intended to.

Because this is the real challenge: if our ultimate aim is to identify the best and brightest talent, and give them access to the best and most useful opportunities in college and graduate school and beyond, so that they may advance to the best and most influential levels of leadership, we have to be able to find some way of identifying talent that controls for the many variables, differences, and disadvantages that permeate the system that brings them to the doors of our institutions.

Affirmative action tried to do that in college and university admissions. What began as an effort to undo the legacy of Jim Crow racism expanded to become an effort to use ethnicity as a proxy for a larger range of underrepresented groups and therefore to expand the aperture of our campus populations beyond its traditional bounds of the mostly white and mostly wealthy. It helped, to a degree (as did, arguably much more so, the GI Bill). But as the Opportunity Insights data show, it didn't help nearly enough, not at the top of the prestige ladder.

And now affirmative action has been ended by a transformed (and transformative) Supreme Court.

For administrators at colleges and universities that used affirmative action who have spent decades refining admissions policies in response to consistent (if periodically refined) legal precedent, 2023's decisions in the *Students for Fair Admissions* cases are bringing about sudden and unwelcome change. (It's worth pausing to note that this is a relatively small number of schools. Most American students don't have to worry about college admission: despite these debates, only 6 percent of U.S. students attend a college with an admission rate under 25 percent.[6])

But perhaps it also creates an opportunity.

"Many universities have for too long wrongly concluded that the touchstone of an individual's identity is not challenges bested, skills built, or lessons learned, but the color of their skin," wrote Chief Justice John Roberts in his decision striking down affirmative action. "This Nation's constitutional history does not tolerate that choice."[7]

The question I ask is, How can we seize this moment to build a better meritocracy, one that recognizes our world as it is, the many, many moments and points at which the notion of meritocracy is undermined, and works to create an admissions and opportunity structure that does indeed recognize challenges bested, skills built, and lessons learned?

When every student has such a wildly different starting line, we need to make the race about not who gets to the finish line first but rather how far they have run.

In fact, the easy thing to do is, essentially, to stereotype, to impute certain characteristics to certain applicants based on where they grew up, or their family background, or their immigration status. And the easy thing to do is to do it once, when they're applying to college, and then declare the problem addressed.

What is better—better for individual students, better for the campus communities we're trying to build, better for society at large, better for accessing the best of American talent—is also much more ambitious and much more expensive.

We need to invest to address inequities throughout the educational system, we need to both work to address inequities and remain mindful that they'll never be fully addressed, and we need corporate America to do its part, too, by opening its recruiting doors to a far wider range of schools, especially in wake of the Supreme Court decision.

We need a much bigger investment in K–12 education in this country, so that the difference in educational quality between wealthy school districts and less wealthy ones, both in terms of academics and in terms of the extracurriculars offered—a big part of what explains the overrepresentation of wealthy families in the Ivy Plus schools—is diminished. Colleges and universities can help by building pipeline programs in partnership with local high schools or schools from which they would like to increase enrollment, helping to support academic achievement and eventual successful applications.

We will need recognition in our college admissions offices that not all students will have access to the same kinds of academic opportunities—or to lacrosse camps or summer trips to the Galapagos—and those offices must seek out ways to identify talent in places with fewer resources, those students who have run longer distances from farther starting lines.

At the same time, college admissions processes will need to change more generally. Test-optional admission, which necessarily grew in prevalence during the pandemic, is increasingly becoming a norm and will likely become even more so in the wake of the Supreme Court's affirmative action decision. As Lemann notes, high school GPAs can be better indicators of college performance, and in any case removing the faux-objective metrics will make it easier for admissions officers to have more flexibility in shaping their classes under this new jurisprudence. In response to that change, and in recognition of Chief Justice Roberts's cryptic guidance in his *Students for Fair Admissions* decision that "nothing in this opinion should be construed as prohibiting universities from considering an applicant's discussion of how race affected his or her life, be it through discrimination, inspiration, or otherwise," ambitious students will work even harder to build individualized cases for themselves—which means admissions offices will need to devote even more resources to careful reading and review of applications.[8]

Colleges and universities will also be likely to give increased focus to building admissions regimes that aim to increase socioeconomic diversity among their incoming classes, as remains constitutionally permissible, a cause that has been advocated by the scholar Richard Kahlenberg since his 1996 book *The Remedy: Class, Race, and Affirmative Action*. (Kahlenberg was an expert witness for the plaintiffs in the recent affirmative action cases.)

We will need more college counselors to help first-generation and low-income students navigate the application process, recognizing that applying to college is a test and trial of its own, and having parents who have done it successfully confers its own legacy advantage. And similarly, we need more college advisers to help first-generation and low-income students succeed once they're matriculated.

And as I have said, we'll need to count on corporate America, too. Part of our successful strategy in the 2003 affirmative action cases at the University of Michigan were the amicus briefs filed by corporate and military leaders attesting to the importance of educating a diverse leadership class. "In order to cultivate a set of leaders with legitimacy in the eyes of the citizenry, it is necessary that the path to leadership be visibly open to talented and qualified individuals of every race and ethnicity," Justice Sandra Day O'Connor wrote in her decision for the court. "All members of our heterogeneous society must have confidence in the openness and integrity of the educational institutions that provide this training."[9]

In order to cultivate that set of leaders, corporations will need to do their part. They can invest in some of the initiatives I described. They can leverage their recruitment and talent development resources to help colleges and universities prepare diverse talents for the careers of the future. And, again recognizing that the playing fields will never be equal, and that there are a lot of brilliant and creative students who don't have the good fortune to be born into the kind of wealth and opportunity that sets them on a glide path to the Ivy League, top corporations can and should become far more expansive in the colleges and universities from which they recruit.

This is a big, growing, and increasingly diverse country. Slightly more than two million bachelor's degrees will be awarded this year,[10] a tiny fraction of them from the Ivy Plus colleges. To make our meritocracy live up to its promise, and keep it distinct from an aristocracy, we must use this moment to make it stronger and more equitable—and we need employers to do their part.

The Multiple Lives and Ironies of the SAT

Prudence L. Carter

WHEN THE CORONAVIRUS PANDEMIC hit the world in 2020, admissions at U.S. colleges and universities pivoted and became "test-optional" to acknowledge the pandemic's adverse impact on SAT preparation and accessibility. Even the most selective ones—the "Ivy Plus" schools[1]—did it; and as a result, their application pools diversified and the number of applications soared exponentially. With MIT taking the lead in 2022, one by one the Ivy Pluses are starting to reverse course. While Harvard has deferred its decision until 2026, Dartmouth, Yale, and Brown have all rededicated themselves recently to the value of one of higher education's bluntest contemporary tools of inequality.

Economists at Opportunity Insights, a big-data research operation based at Harvard, have examined all SAT and ACT test takers in the United States from 2011, 2013, and 2015 and linked their scores to their families' tax records. They found a

strong linear and positive relationship among the quintile levels of household income and the percentage of students who
score 1300 or above on the SAT—a threshold that is likely to
merit admission to the Ivy Plus universities, including Stanford, MIT, and the University of California, Berkeley. The differences widen as the students' families move higher up the
income ladder.[2] Students whose household incomes fall
within the top 20 percent of all income groups are *seven* times
more likely to score a 1300 or above than those from families
in the bottom 20 percent of household income. These researchers have shown unequivocally that the SAT reproduces
class (and by close correlation, racial) inequality in the United
States. We know little about how much tutoring and test preparation services actually determine the disproportionate share
of high scorers among the affluent. Undeniably, wealthier
families are more likely to afford access to resources that can
lift SAT scores, and we have some indication of the demand
for test preparation in the United States, whose market is ex-
pected to grow by nearly $15 billion between 2022 and 2027.[3]

Decades ago, I was a naive high school junior operating
under the assumption that very high academic achievement
and a demonstrable effort reflected in a strong grade point average were sufficient for entry into college. I knew that either
the ACT or the SAT was required for admission, but I under-
estimated their significance greatly. Many, particularly those
whose families, like mine, are unfamiliar with the intricacies
of elite colleges and universities, remain unaware of the pivotal
role they play, especially in selective institutions. The true
weight of the SAT became evident to me on the other side of
a four-year bachelor's degree while I worked as an admissions

officer at my alma mater, an Ivy League university. Then I began to observe how higher education officials gauged students' intelligence, competence, and potential for academic success based on a relatively crude indicator of potential.

Nicholas Lemann, an accomplished journalist and a leading thinker in education, purveys some of the foundational history of both the SAT and higher education in his new book, *Higher Admissions.* In the mid-twentieth century, Harvard University president James Bryant Conant aspired to broaden educational opportunity to white males who were not only the sons of the patrician New England classes attending boarding schools but who were also from other social classes in a relatively young republic. In his deft narrative ability, Lemann characterizes Conant as someone who aimed to reduce the power and sway of the wealthiest Americans on the nation's most esteemed university and who wanted to cast a wider net of opportunity for the white men whose parents could not afford to send them to private boarding schools. Accordingly, Conant introduced a scholarship program for lower-income students and charged an assistant dean, Henry Chauncey, with the task of locating an "aptitude" test that would show that intelligence was broadly distributed across social classes of white men.

Summarizing the timeline further, Lemann shares that Chauncey found Princeton University professor Carl Brigham, "who had worked on the first mass administration of an IQ test, to U.S. Army inductees in the First World War and had gone on to produce an adaptation of that test for college admissions purposes. Brigham called it the Scholastic Aptitude Test."[4] Brigham had already piloted the test experimentally in

1926, and based on Conant's charge and Chauncey's search for a test, Harvard adopted Brigham's test for its new scholarship program. Over time, Conant and Chauncey persuaded other universities to get rid of their other exams and instead incorporate this early forebear of today's SAT as the main admissions test. Both Conant and Chauncey perceived that they were delivering the United States from a plutocracy to a democracy by utilizing an instrument that could separate the "intellectually superior" across all white male social classes from the average and less capable. Eventually Chauncey left Harvard, writes Lemann, to establish the Educational Testing Service (ETS). The SAT, once created and marketed, took on subsequent and multiple lives of its own. It would eventually become one of the defining allocation tools of opportunity in American higher education. Having experienced multiple reincarnations, including a name change, the SAT has now played a crucial role in shaping the trajectories of countless individuals, or as Lemann declares, "affecting the high school experience of many more people who aren't selected for elite colleges than people who are selected."[5]

The debate surrounding the SAT and its implications for racial and class differences in higher education highlights a complex web of social, economic, and educational dynamics. The preference for the SAT among selective colleges and universities underscores its role not only as a measure of academic readiness but also as a gatekeeper of opportunity. Achieving high scores can be seen as possessing what sociologists refer to as "cultural capital," a resource signaling a student's readiness and worthiness to attend prestigious schools, which will likely lead to better economic opportunities. The ETS and

the test preparation industry play a significant role in legitimiz-
ing and reinforcing the SAT's importance through marketing
and branding efforts. These efforts not only sell the test to students, families, schools, and institutions but also contribute to
the narrative that high SAT scores are essential for academic
and, ultimately, professional success. Thus, the resilience of the
SAT, despite criticism and calls for a more holistic approach
to college admissions, reflects its embeddedness within the
dominant cultural mindset, as well as structures of higher education and its intersection with broader societal values around
merit, achievement, and success.

Ironically, contrary to Conant's and Chauncey's initial in-
tent to make Harvard accessible to diverse classes of white
men—and by extension other elite colleges and universities—
the SAT has evolved into a reproducer of inequality in higher
education.

People of color and women, whom Lemann writes less
about, did not prefigure into Conant's calculation. Yet, higher
education's mission and reach evolved across the late twentieth century, especially in response to the demands of the civil
rights movement. U.S. democracy grew into a relatively more
inclusive one where individuals whom the original colonizers
and national builders had barely considered human, such as
various racial and ethnic groups, women, and girls, began to
have some access to higher education.

A critical mass of descendants of the colonized, the en-
slaved, and those who confronted other forms of subjugation
has joined these institutions since the 1960s and 1970s. Yet,
with the SAT's evolution across time, levels of strong, enduring
relative educational inequality have maintained their stubborn-

ness. That is, absolute changes in representation or diversity in selective higher education's social demographics have not elided the conspicuously strong *relative* inequalities in access to these educational "goods" and opportunities between certain groups. While affirmative action practices have benefited women, especially those who are white, and racial minorities in selective colleges and universities, the intersections of economic and educational opportunity and social categorization bode less well for African Americans, Latinx, and Indigenous peoples. Affirmative action practices in higher education have yielded significantly different outcomes by race and gender over time.[6]

As a sociologist and educational researcher, I have examined in depth how U.S. inequality engenders persistent learning disparities by race, class, and gender. Some refer to them as "achievement gaps"; my colleagues and I refer to them as "opportunity gaps,"[7] which produce racial and class-based disparities not only in test scores but also in college-going and attainment rates. Scores of studies and decades of research from social scientists across multiple disciplines indicate that to create an even chance of success for most American learners, our leaders would need to address the core needs of children and families, from livable wages for families to affordable housing and health care to high-quality teaching and learning in culturally rich (and sustaining) schools.[8]

In our coedited volume *Closing the Opportunity Gap: What America Must Do to Give Every Child an Even Chance*,[9] Kevin Welner and I argued from an ecological perspective—with knowledge of the resources to which most middle- and upper-class children have access—that opportunity gaps both inside and outside of schools, from teacher quality, funding, classroom size, and high-quality preschool to family income, housing, and community resources, among other factors, drive achievement gaps. We were not arguing that a student had to reach a particular threshold in every one of these domains, but social science data are clear that middle- and upper-class learners whose families possess resources in nearly all of them actualize better outcomes just about anywhere.[10]

As I have delved more deeply into this multidimensional framework of the "ecology of inequality" and its threat to the health of our democracy, the main question has become: How do we gain stronger traction on the broader societal policies and practices needed to provide equitable opportunity and education for historically racially and economically disadvantaged young people? Though the direction of public education has been mainly left to states' jurisdiction, reform has often been embedded in national policy drivers such as the Elementary and Secondary Education Act of 1965 (ESEA), a critical piece of the Great Society's War on Poverty to improve educational opportunities for children from poor families. In 2001, the No Child Left Behind Act (NCLB) was passed and ceded the matter of reduction of educational disparities among students to a mandate for states, districts, and schools to reduce test score gaps. Presumably, if students, especially racially minoritized, English Language Learners, and low-income learners, grew their test score proficiency, then no child could be left behind in terms of educational mobility. Targeted goals for test score performances for specific student groups were not only unattainable by the mandated year (2014) but also not necessarily ameliorative in terms of the wider goals embedded within the original ESEA.[11]

No amount of reform, my colleagues and I have argued, will reduce educational inequality and racial disparities without some assurance that all students have the fundamental right to a strong, equitable education. Similarly, Lemann declares: "Every American child should have a decent public education that leaves him or her truly literate, numerate, and able to think and act as an empowered citizen."[12] Reforming the inequities in U.S. K–12 education is a tall albeit not insurmountable order. It requires appropriate, as opposed to minimal, attention to macroeconomic and social conditions that impact students' lives inside and outside of schools, from home and community resources to high-quality pedagogy and educators in terms of facility with both subject matter and broader sociological competencies regarding race, class, gender, and history and the cultural ethos of K–12 schools, colleges, and universities (e.g., social climate, inclusion and belonging). The forms of capital in children's lives matter significantly, from economic to cultural and social. Further, let's not forget about the extent to which those resources can be further enhanced, as mentioned earlier, by access to additional resources such as private tutors and testing prep services that affluent families can afford for their children.[13]

Meanwhile, limited selective college admissions slots have stoked intense competition among families across the nation. Commonly, families make housing decisions based on the public school options available to them, and our state and national systems have bred this competition through grades and "Exemplary School" monikers awarded to schools based on their aggregate students' test scores. Parents seek returns on their housing investments in public school districts with schools labeled as high achieving, if available. Otherwise, they enroll their children in either private or independent schools, which can meet their perceived needs. (I cannot judge and must admit that I live in one of those complicit families.)

Many parents invest additional resources to enhance their children's chances of attaining either a good or a better life. For many, the good life entails acceptances at high-status colleges and universities. Consequently, it is the norm for upwardly mobile families to "play the game" and embrace cultural logics and values institutionalized to determine academic success and mobility, including attending high-quality schools, getting high grades, participating in numerous extracurricular activities, and obtaining stratospheric SAT or ACT test scores. In turn, the consumption of education for the public good in the early twentieth century has developed into education as a private good—one for individual or personal interests and increasingly less a good that ensures the health of an inclusive democracy.[14] Competitive middle- and upper-class parents and students who treat education primarily as a private good, whether unintentionally or not, disregard the reasons why history has demanded corrective, redistributive practices. Consequently, they now either willingly or tacitly accept racial and socioeconomic segregation in their communities. When Conant and Chauncey conspired to create an aptitude test that would open the doors to Harvard in the 1940s to build a more representative (white male) leadership class and intelligentsia, as Nicholas Lemann shares with us, they believed that they were doing a good thing for the nation.

The persistence of the myth of meritocracy, coupled with the perpetuation of deficit narratives surrounding under-achieving, poor, working-class, and supposedly "less quali-fied" Black, Indigenous, and Latinx students, forms a barrier to accepting educational policies aimed at rectifying past dis-crimination and fostering equity. Even if these students dem-onstrate excellence within their communities, the reliance on SAT scores—benchmarked against averages inflated by more privileged peers—can effectively exclude them from the top-tier colleges and universities, particularly those that continue to mandate SAT scores for admissions.

Adding a layer of historical irony, in June 2023 the U.S. Supreme Court created a full-circle moment. The test whose origins trace back to Harvard University in the early twentieth century ultimately played a role in dismantling the same uni-versity's liberal, race-based holistic admissions process less than a century later. Affirmative action, much like K–12 school integration, has faced erosion because the promotion of racial diversity in schools and education is not deemed a compelling national interest for the majority in America. This sentiment is underscored by a 2019 Pew Research poll revealing that a significant majority of (white) Americans express a preference for local schools over diverse ones.[15]

Lemann's book concludes on a mildly somber note, just as this response is likely to do. The question is where we go from here in a nation where there is no federal or state guarantee of a high-quality education for all students to really approxi-mate a more level field of education. An ultimate challenge lies in addressing the majority of U.S. students for whom the SAT is not a pivotal aspect of the high-stakes college admissions game affecting only around 6 percent of college-bound students. Ironically, the very issues that spurred the call for equal opportunity in education for marginalized youth in the early twentieth century persist, shaping patterns of achievement disparities a century later. The enduring forces of racism and economic inequality infiltrate the walls of schools across the nation's thirteen thousand districts and significantly inhibit equal opportunity for all social groups in higher education.

Meanwhile, the future of both K–12 and higher education, driven by technological advancements, will be quite different from anything most of us could have imagined. The World Economic Forum's (WEF) *Future of Jobs Report 2023* forecasts significant changes during the period from 2023 to 2027, with significant declines in some labor segments and increases in others due to artificial intelligence and big data analytics.[16] While machines may excel in certain areas, conveying emotional intelligence remains a uniquely human capability, essential in both work and daily life. Our society continues to require what education historian David Tyack called the "humanization of industry."[17]

Moreover, the imperative for environmental sustainability, driven by the challenges of climate change and global warming, underscores the need for expansion in the agricultural, vocational education, and digital commerce sectors. Our planet urgently requires a generation of residents and learners who will pioneer innovations in renewable energy, contributing to the preservation rather than the detriment of the earth. The WEF's report highlights that future work demands skills such as analytical and creative thinking, empathy, active listening, leadership, and influence. Notably, these skills are crucial for addressing the complex challenges posed by rapid technological advancements and environmental sustainability. Traditional metrics like the SAT, now susceptible to being outperformed by artificial intelligence embodied in machines, will fall short in assessing these essential skills.[18]

Lemann writes persuasively that "Just as it's an illusion to believe that standardized admissions tests for highly selective colleges represent opportunity in America, it's also an illusion to believe that dropping these tests will bring about the dawn of a new age of truly meaningful equal opportunity in America." He ends by noting that the fix for equalizing American education requires "a different project, much larger, and far more important."[19] Lemann acknowledges the necessity for change. Yet, he stops short of offering any concrete visions or solutions.

The urgency for both K–12 and higher education reform cannot be overstressed. A democratic society, with higher education as one of its pillars, has a responsibility to nurture the boundless potential of a diverse new generation of thinkers and producers, regardless of their social backgrounds. Considering the evolving landscape of technology and significant changes in the labor market, a reliance on the SAT for admissions might be increasingly misaligned with the exigencies of the future, including the determination of the next generation of leaders and policymakers. We must ask ourselves whether we are missing a pivotal moment for a re-envisioned approach to selecting the minds who will shape the future. Paradoxically, a deadly pandemic offered an opportune moment for our higher education system—especially the modest-sized sector of highly selective colleges and universities—to transcend their historical reliance on metrics that further entrench social and economic divides. For pragmatic reasons of ease and efficiency, or the desire for "objective" measures of academic potential, in addition to the dominance of the cultural logics that we construct about the "chosen,"[20] some of these institutions are now returning to old practices rather than engaging in deeper introspection to ensure that their practices truly align with the institutions' professed values of accessibility and inclusion. Meanwhile, the actualization of a collective future within a truly representative, democratic fabric hinges on this critical alignment of principles and actions.

Notes

Introduction

1. Ray Hart et al., *Student Testing in America's Great City Schools: An Inventory and Preliminary Analysis* (Washington, DC: Council of the Great City Schools, October 2015), https://www.cgcs.org/cms/lib/DC00001581/Centricity/Domain/87/Testing%20Report.pdf.

2. Nancy Burton, *Predicting Success in College: SAT Studies of Classes Graduating since 1980* (College Board Research Report No. 2001-2) (Princeton, NJ: Educational Testing Service, 2001).

3. See Rebecca Zwick, ed., *Rethinking the SAT: The Future of Standardized Testing in University Admissions* (London: Routledge, 2004), esp. Geiser and Studley, "Predictive Validity and Differential Impact of the SAT I and SAT II at the University of California."

4. Claire Cain Miller, "New SAT Data Highlights the Deep Inequality at the Heart of American Education," *New York Times*, October 23, 2023.

5. Claude Steele, *Whistling Vivaldi: How Stereotypes Affect Us and What We Can Do* (New York: W. W. Norton, 2010).

6. Gary Orfield, *The Walls around Opportunity: The Failure of Colorblind Policy for Higher Education* (Princeton, NJ: Princeton University Press, 2022), esp. chap. 1.

7. William H. Frey, "The 'Diversity Explosion' Is America's Twenty-First-Century Baby Boom," in *Our Compelling Interests: The Value of Diversity for Democracy and a Prosperous Society*, ed. Earl Lewis and Nancy Cantor (Princeton, NJ: Princeton University Press, 2016), 16–38.

8. Earl Lewis, "Toward a 2.0 Compact for the Liberal Arts," *Daedalus* 148, no. 4 (Fall 2019): 218–221; Evan Castilo and Lyss Welding, "Closed Colleges: List, Statistics,

and Major Closures," Best Colleges, January 17, 2024, https://www.bestcolleges
.com/research/closed-colleges-list-statistics-major-closures/.

9. See the report *Higher Education for American Democracy: A Report of the President's Commission on Higher Education*, 6 vols. (Washington, DC: Government Printing Office, 1947), https://books.google.com/books/about/Higher
_Education_for_American_Democracy.html?id=wvCcAAAAMAAJ.

10. University of California, Office of the President, "Institutional Research and Academic Planning," accessed February 21, 2024, https://www.ucop.edu
/institutional-research-academic-planning/content-analysis/academic-planning
/california-master-plan.html.

11. For a description of the key components, see University of Maryland, Baltimore County, "Meyerhoff Scholars Program," accessed February 21, 2024, https://
meyerhoff.umbc.edu/13-key-components/.

12. Alicia Victoria Lozano, "California Ends Affirmative Action in the '90s but Retains a Diverse Student Body," NBC News, June 29, 2023, https://www.nbcnews
.com/news/us-news/california-ended-affirmative-action-90s-retains-diverse
-student-body-rcna91846.

13. California saw a noticeable dip in racial diversity in the University of California system after the adoption of Proposition 209 but has seen enhanced diversification of late. Patricia Gándara attributes this to policies and practices, especially the cessation of requiring the SAT.

14. For a full accounting of this argument, see the briefs filed in the complaint and briefs filed in the *Grutter* and *Gratz* cases. The litigants conceded that all of the students admitted to the University of Michigan were qualified. They steadfastly objected to any consideration of race.

15. Scott E. Page, *The Diversity Bonus: How Great Teams Pay Off in the Knowledge Economy* (Princeton, NJ: Princeton University Press, 2017).

16. David Leonhardt, "The Misguided War on the SAT," *New York Times*, January 7, 2024.

1. The Birth of the American Meritocracy

1. W. Allison Davis and Robert Havighurst, "The Measurement of Mental Systems (Can Intelligence Be Measured?)," *Scientific Monthly* 66, no. 4 (1948): 307, 311.

2. Henry Chauncey, notebook entry for July 31, 1948, Henry Chauncey Papers, Box 95, Folder 1068, Frame 00250, Educational Testing Service Archives, Princeton, NJ (hereafter Henry Chauncey Papers).

3. Carl C. Brigham, *A Study of American Intelligence* (Princeton, NJ: Princeton University Press, 1923), 190.

4. Carl Brigham, "Intelligence Tests of Immigrant Groups," *Psychological Review* 37, no. 2 (1930); Brigham, "Manuscript for Article on Board Examinations Taken by West Point and Annapolis," handwritten, dated 1934–35, Carl Campbell Brigham Papers, Box 1, Folder labeled "MSS 4," 17, Educational Testing Service Archives, Princeton, NJ.

5. It's worth noting that when Conant was a Harvard undergraduate, Frederick Jackson Turner, the originator of the now much-disputed "frontier thesis" of American history, was a highly esteemed faculty member there.

6. James B. Conant, "Wanted: American Radicals," *Atlantic Monthly*, May 1943.

7. Henry Chauncey, letter to the editor of the *Boston Globe*, February 12, 1945, Henry Chauncey Papers, Box 47, Folder 1041.

2. Higher Education for All

1. U.S. President's Commission on Higher Education, *Higher Education for American Democracy: A Report of the President's Commission on Higher Education*, 6 vols. (Washington, DC: Government Printing Office, 1947), https://books .google.com/books/about/Higher_Education_for_American_Democracy.html ?id=wvCcAAAAMAAJ, 1:65.

2. U.S. President's Commission on Higher Education, *Higher Education for American Democracy*, 2:6.

3. An excellent overview of this subject, pre–standardized testing, is Harold S. Weschsler, *The Qualified Student: A History of Selective College Admission in America* (New York: John Wiley and Sons, 1977). Much of my discussion of the early days of college admissions is drawn from it.

4. Roger L. Geiger, *The History of American Higher Education: Learning and Culture from the Founding to World War II* (Princeton, NJ: Princeton University Press, 2015), 282.

5. Lawrence Vesey, *The Emergence of the American University* (1965; Chicago: University of Chicago Press, 1970), 13–14.

6. E. F. Lindquist, ed., *Educational Measurement* (Washington, DC: American Council on Education, 1951), 8, 16, 37.

7. Clark Kerr, *The Uses of the University*, 3rd ed. (1963; Cambridge, MA: Harvard University Press, 1982), 121. See also John W. Gardner, *Excellence: Can We Be Equal and Excellent Too?* (New York: Harper, 1961). Gardner was the president of the

Carnegie Corporation, a trustee of ETS, and another crucial supporter of the SAT. Both Kerr and Gardner shared with Conant a conviction that educational elitism must be zealously protected and that this can be done without peril to the larger dream of an egalitarian society.

3. Testing, Affirmative Action, and the Law

1. W. Allison Davis and Robert Havighurst, "The Measurement of Mental Systems (Can Intelligence Be Measured?)," *Scientific Monthly* 66, no. 4 (1948): 301–316.

2. William O. Douglas, dissenting opinion in DeFunis v. Odegaard, 416 U.S. 312 (1974).

3. Robert Comfort, interview with the author, April 12, 2021.

4. John C. Jeffries, *Justice Lewis F. Powell Jr. and the Era of Judicial Balance* (New York: Scribner, 1994), 487.

5. The 1947 Truman Commission report, *Higher Education for American Democracy*, uses the word "diversity" repeatedly, both in describing the state of American higher education and as a quality to be desired, as in "We need to perceive the rich advantages of cultural diversity."

6. A standard anecdote from pretesting days entails a professor saying on the first day of class, "Look to your right. Look to your left. One of the three of you won't be here next year."

7. James Bierman, interview with the author, March 3, 2021.

8. Marginal note by Lewis Powell in Regents of University of California v. Bakke, Supreme Court Case Files Collection, Box 469–472, Powell Papers, Lewis F. Powell Jr. Archives, Washington and Lee University School of Law, Lexington, VA.

9. *The Open Universities in South Africa* (n.p.: Witwatersrand University Press, 1957), 6, 14–15.

10. *The Open Universities in South Africa*, 14.

11. Thomas J. Espenshade and Alexandra Walton Radford, *No Longer Separate, Not Yet Equal: Race and Class in Elite College Admission and College Life* (Princeton, NJ: Princeton University Press, 2009), 92; *Report of the UC University Academic Council Standardized Testing Task Force*, Systemwide Academic Council, University of California, January 2020, 45.

12. Jamal Greene, *How Rights Went Wrong: Why Our Obsession with Rights Is Tearing America Apart* (Boston: Houghton Mifflin Harcourt, 2021), 201.

13. Michael J. Sandel, *Liberalism and the Limits of Justice* (Cambridge: Cambridge University Press, 1982), 141.

14. Robert Comfort, interview with the author.

15. In his 2023 majority decision striking down affirmative action, Chief Justice John Roberts included an unexplained footnote exempting the military academies, which can still take race into account in admissions.

16. Sandra Day O'Connor, majority opinion in Grutter v. Bollinger, 539 U.S. 306 (2003).

17. Evan Thomas, *First: Sandra Day O'Connor* (New York: Random House, 2019).

18. Samuel Alito, dissenting opinion in Fisher v. University of Texas, 579 U.S. 365 (2016).

4. Admissions without Testing

1. Richard C. Atkinson and David S. Saxon, "Standardized Tests and Access to American Universities: February 2001," in *The Pursuit of Knowledge: Speeches and Papers of Richard C. Atkinson*, ed. Patricia A. Pelfrey (Berkeley: University of California Press, 2007), 137–148.

2. This seems to have been mainly a business decision: not enough colleges were requiring the SAT II, and therefore not enough students were taking it, to generate enough revenue to make it worthwhile to the College Board.

3. Anthony Carnevale, interview with the author, November 30, 2022.

4. William G. Bowen, Matthew M. Chingos, and Michael S. McPherson, *Crossing the Finish Line: Completing College at America's Public Universities* (Princeton, NJ: Princeton University Press, 2009), 115–116.

5. Testing without Meritocracy

1. Leo Tolstoy, *War and Peace* (1869), Book Six, Chapter Five.

2. Joseph F. Kett, *Merit: The History of a Founding Ideal from the American Revolution to the Twenty-First Century* (Ithaca, NY: Cornell University Press, 2013), 97.

3. Lester J. Cappon, ed., *The Adams-Jefferson Letters: The Complete Correspondence between Thomas Jefferson and Abigail and John Adams* (Chapel Hill: University of North Carolina Press, 1959), 388.

4. Cappon, *The Adams-Jefferson Letters*, 400.

5. Raj Chetty, David J. Deming, and John N. Friedman, "Diversifying Society's Leaders? The Determinants and Causal Effects of Admission to Highly Selective Private Colleges," October 2023, 1, 2, https://opportunityinsights.org/wp-content/uploads/2023/07/CollegeAdmissions_Paper.pdf.

6. Chetty, Deming, and Friedman, "Diversifying Society's Leaders?," 140.

7. College Board, *2023 SAT Suite of Assessments Annual Report*, 7, accessed March 31, 2024, https://reports.collegeboard.org/media/pdf/2023-total-group-sat-suite-of-assessments-annual-report%20ADA.pdf.

8. Chetty, Deming, and Friedman, "Diversifying Society's Leaders?," 87.

9. Anthony P. Carnevale, Ban Cheah, and Emma Wenzinger, *The College Payoff: More Education Doesn't Always Mean More Earnings*, 6, accessed March 31, 2024, https://repository.library.georgetown.edu/bitstream/handle/10822/1062946/cew-college_payoff_2021-fr.pdf?sequence=1&isAllowed=y.

10. E. F. Lindquist, ed., *Educational Measurement* (Washington, DC: American Council on Education, 1951), 47.

11. Richard C. Atkinson, "College Admissions and the SAT: A Personal Perspective," Association for Psychological Science, May 24, 2005, https://www.psychologicalscience.org/observer/college-admissions-and-the-sat-a-personal-perspective.

Commentary: Higher Admissions, a California Perspective

1. Educational Testing Service, *2014 ETS Standards for Quality and Fairness* (Princeton, NJ: Educational Testing Service, 2015), 62.

2. Patricia Gándara and Elias López, "Latino Students and College Entrance Exams: How Much Do They Really Matter?," *Hispanic Journal of Behavioral Sciences* 20, no. 1 (1998): 17–38.

3. Teresa Watanabe, "UC's Record-Smashing Applications Put Long-Held Diversity Goals within Reach," *Los Angeles Times*, January 29, 2021, https://www.latimes.com/california/story/2021-01-29/uc-record-college-admission-applications-show-wide-diversity.

4. This began as the top 10 percent plan at the University of Texas but has since been reduced to 6 percent, and is as high as 50 percent at some Texas colleges.

5. For example, "special talents" includes achievements and awards in a particular field, such as visual and performing arts, communication, or athletic endeavors; special skills, such as demonstrated written and oral proficiency in other languages; special interests, such as intensive study and exploration of other cultures; experiences that demonstrate unusual promise for leadership, such as significant community service or significant participation in student government; or other significant experiences or achievements that demonstrate the student's promise for contributing to the intellectual vitality of a campus.

6. Rebecca Zwick citing Sen (2000) in "The Role of Standardized Tests in College Admissions" (Los Angeles: Civil Rights Project, June 8, 2023), https://civilrightsproject.ucla.edu/news/research/college-access/admissions/the-role-of-standardized-tests-in-college-admissions.

Commentary: The Future of the Meritocracy

1. Michael Young, *The Rise of the Meritocracy, 1870–2033: An Essay on Education and Equality* (London: Thames and Hudson, 1958).

2. Aatish Bhatia, Claire Cain Miller, and Josh Katz, "Study of Elite College Admissions Data Suggests Being Very Rich Is Its Own Qualification," *New York Times*, July 24, 2023, https://www.nytimes.com/interactive/2023/07/24/upshot/ivy-league-elite-college-admissions.html.

3. Raj Chetty, David J. Deming, and John N. Friedman, "Diversifying Society's Leaders? The Determinants and Causal Effects of Admission to Highly Selective Private Colleges," October 2023, 1–3, https://opportunityinsights.org/wp-content/uploads/2023/07/CollegeAdmissions_Paper.pdf. Emphasis added.

4. Richard V. Reeves, *Dream Hoarders: How the American Upper Middle Class Is Leaving Everyone Else in the Dust, Why That Is a Problem, and What to Do about It* (Washington, DC: Brookings Institution Press, 2017), 12, https://www.brookings.edu/books/dream-hoarders/.

5. Reeves, *Dream Hoarders*, 146–147.

6. Richard Arum and Mitchell L. Stevens, "For Most College Students, Affirmative Action Was Never Enough," *New York Times*, July 3, 2023, https://www.nytimes.com/interactive/2023/07/03/opinion/for-most-college-students-affirmative-action-was-not-enough.html.

7. Students for Fair Admissions, Inc. v. President and Fellows of Harvard College, No. 20-1199, slip op. at 8 (U.S. June 29, 2023), https://www.supremecourt.gov/opinions/22pdf/20-1199_hgdj.pdf.

8. Students for Fair Admissions, Inc. v. President and Fellows of Harvard College, 39.

9. Grutter v. Bollinger et al., 539 U.S. 306, 334 (2003), https://tile.loc.gov/storage-services/service/ll/usrep/usrep539/usrep539306/usrep539306.pdf.

10. William J. Hussar and Tabitha M. Bailey, *Projections of Education Statistics to 2024*, 43rd ed. (Washington, DC: Government Printing Office, 2016), 66, https://nces.ed.gov/pubs2016/2016013.pdf.

Commentary: The Multiple Lives
and Ironies of the SAT

1. The Ivy Plus schools are considered the eight Ivy League universities (Brown, Columbia, Cornell, Dartmouth, Harvard, the University of Pennsylvania, Princeton, and Yale) and several other highly selective universities, including CalTech, the University of Chicago, Duke, Georgetown, Johns Hopkins, MIT, Northwestern, Rice, Stanford, and Washington University (Missouri).

2. Claire Cain Miller, "New SAT Data Highlights the Deep Inequality at the Heart of American Education," *New York Times*, October 23, 2023, https://www.nytimes.com/interactive/2023/10/23/upshot/sat-inequality.html.

3. "US Test Preparation Market Size to Grow by USD 14.72 Billion from 2022 to 2027: ArborBridge Inc., BenchPrep, Blackboard Inc., and MORE to Be Key Players of the Market–Technavio," Yahoo Finance, October 9, 2023, https://finance.yahoo.com/news/us-test-preparation-market-size-183000728.html.

4. See Nicholas Lemann, "The Birth of the American Meritocracy," chapter 1 in this volume.

5. See Nicholas Lemann, "Admissions without Testing," chapter 4 in this volume.

6. Prudence L. Carter, "Unrealized Integration in Education, Sociology, and Society," *American Sociological Review* 89, no. 1 (2004): 6–30.

7. Prudence L. Carter and Kevin G. Welner, eds., *Closing the Opportunity Gap: What America Must Do to Give Every Child an Even Chance* (New York: Oxford University Press, 2013).

8. Greg J. Duncan and Richard I. Murnane, eds., *Whither Opportunity? Rising Inequality, Schools, and Children's Life Chances* (New York: Russell Sage Foundation, 2011).

9. Carter and Welner, *Closing the Opportunity Gap*.

10. Douglas S. Massey, Camile Z. Charles, Garvey F. Lundy, and Mary J. Fischer, *The Source of the River: The Social Origins of Freshmen at America's Selective Colleges and Universities* (Princeton, NJ: Princeton University Press, 2003).

11. Linda Darling-Hammond, "Race, Inequality and Educational Accountability: The Irony of 'No Child Left Behind,'" *Race Ethnicity and Education* 10, no. 3 (2007): 245–260.

12. See Nicholas Lemann, "Testing without Meritocracy," chapter 5 in this volume.

13. Sean Drake, *Academic Apartheid: Race and the Criminalization of Failure in an American Suburb* (Berkeley: University of California Press, 2022); Natasha

Warikoo, *Race at the Top: Asian Americans and Whites in Pursuit of the American Dream in Suburban Schools* (Chicago: University of Chicago Press, 2022).

14. David F. Labaree, *Someone Has to Fail: The Zero-Sum Game of Public Schooling* (Cambridge, MA: Harvard University Press, 2011).

15. Juliana Menasce Horowitz, "Americans See Advantages and Challenges in Country's Growing Racial and Ethnic Diversity," Pew Research Center, May 8, 2019, https://www.pewresearch.org/social-trends/2019/05/08/americans-see-advantages-and-challenges-in-countrys-growing- racial-and-ethnic-diversity/.

16. World Economic Forum, *Future of Jobs Report 2023*, May 2023, https://www3.weforum.org/docs/WEF_Future_of_Jobs_2023.pdf.

17. See David Tyack, *The One Best System: A History of American Urban Education* (Cambridge, MA: Harvard University Press, 1974).

18. Ian Bogast, "Is This the Singularity for Standardized Tests?," *The Atlantic*, March 23, 2023, https://www.theatlantic.com/technology/archive/2023/03/open-ai-gpt4-standardized-tests-sat-ap-exams/673458/.

19. See Nicholas Lemann, "Testing without Meritocracy," chapter 5 in this volume.

20. Jerome Karabel, *The Chosen: The Hidden History of Admission and Exclusion at Harvard, Yale, and Princeton* (Boston: Houghton Mifflin, 2005).

Index

Our Compelling Interests

Steering Committee

Anthony Appiah, Professor of Philosophy and Law, New York University

Saleem Badat, Research Professor in History, University of the Free State

Armando I. Bengochea, Senior Program Officer and Director of the Mellon Mays Undergraduate Fellowship Program, The Andrew W. Mellon Foundation

Nancy Cantor, Co-chair, President, Hunter College

Rosario Ceballo, Dean of Georgetown College and Professor of Psychology, Georgetown University

Tabbye Chavous, Vice Provost for Equity & Inclusion and Chief Diversity Officer at the University of Michigan and Professor of Education and Psychology

Sumi Cho, Director of Strategic Initiatives, African American Policy Forum

Angela Dillard, Vice Provost for Undergraduate Education, and Richard A. Meisler Collegiate Professor of Afroamerican and African Studies and History in the College of Literature, Science, and the Arts

Stephanie A. Fryberg, Associate Professor of American Indian Studies and Psychology, University of Washington, and University Diversity and Social Transformation Professor of Psychology, University of Michigan

Patricia Y. Gurin, Nancy Cantor Distinguished University Professor Emerita of Psychology and Women's Studies, University of Michigan

Makeba Morgan Hill, Founder and CEO, Dr. Makeba & Friends, LLC

Earl Lewis, Thomas C. Holt Distinguished University Professor of History, Afroamerican and African Studies and Public Policy, and Director, Center for Social Solutions

Gary Orfield, Distinguished Research Professor of Education, Law, Political Science and Urban Planning and Co-director, Civil Rights Project / Proyecto Derechos Civiles, University of California at Los Angeles

Scott E. Page, John Seely Brown Distinguished University Professor of Complexity, Social Science, and Management, Williamson Family Professor of Business Administration, Professor of Management and Organizations, Political Science, Complex Systems, and Economics, University of Michigan

Eboo Patel, Founder and President, Interfaith America

George J. Sanchez, Professor of American Studies and Ethnicity, and History, University of Southern California

Claude M. Steele, I. James Quillen Endowed Dean, Emeritus, at the Stanford University Graduate School of Education, and Lucie Stern Professor in the Social Sciences, Emeritus, Stanford University

Susan P. Sturm, George M. Jaffin Professor of Law and Social Responsibility, Director of the Center for Institutional and Social Change, Columbia University Law School

Thomas J. Sugrue, Silver Professor of Social and Cultural Analysis and History, Director of the NYU Cities Collaborative, New York University

Beverly Daniel Tatum, President Emerita, Spelman College

Doreen N. Tinajero, Project Senior Manager, Center for Social Solutions, University of Michigan

Sarah E. Turner, University Professor of Economics and Education, Souder Family Professor, University of Virginia

Michele S. Warman, Experienced Practitioner in Residence, Columbia Law School

Laura Washington, President and Chief Executive Officer, Community Foundations of the Hudson Valley

Alford Young Jr., University Diversity and Social Transformation Professor, Edgar G. Epps Collegiate Professor of Sociology, Arthur F. Thurnau Professor of Sociology, Afroamerican and African Studies, and Public Policy, Associate Director, Center for Social Solutions, Faculty Director, Anti-Racism Collaborative, National Center for Institutional Diversity, University of Michigan